Emma Boyes
1,123 Quirky Quotes About Cats

© 2016, Emma Boyes
emmaboyes@gmail.com

With thanks to:

Damon Torsten Nash, Lucy Honeywood and all at
Honeycat Rescue, Lauren Pears and all at Lady
Dinah's Cat Emporium, Rebecca Hall at Nine Lives
Greece, Christina and Joan at Santorini Animal
Welfare Association and everyone who bought
and/or reviewed my last book 1106 Fascinating
Facts About Cats!

Contents

The Joy of Cats

Cats Vs Dogs

Cats and Writers

Crazy Cat People

Cat Haters

Kittens, Kittens, Kittens

Old Cats

After Cats Have Gone

Bedtime...or not

Catnip

Particular Breeds

The Fine Art of Cat Washing

Masters of Relaxation

Mysteriousness

Wild Cats

Purrs, Hisses and Meows

Purrsonalities

Strays

Beautiful Beasts

It's a Cat's Life

The Philosophy of Cats

Proverbially Speaking

Slogans and Puns

Neil Gaiman

Terry Pratchett

Doris Lessing

Margaret Atwood

Catwoman

The Joy of Cats

"There are two means of refuge from the miseries of life: music and cats." - Albert Schweitzer

"I love cats because I enjoy my home; and little by little, they become its visible soul." - Jean Cocteau

"There are few things in life more heartwarming than to be welcomed by a cat." - Tay Hohoff

"I love cats. I even think we have one at home." - Edward L Burlingame

"Once I was gone for a month and I was just miserable, so I flew back from Florida for two hours just to be home and see my cats." - Paula Poundstone

"One small cat changes coming home to an empty house to coming home."- Pam Brown

"I have an Egyptian cat. He leaves a pyramid in every room." - Rodney Dangerfield

"Only cat lovers know the luxury of fur-coated, musical hot-water bottles that don't go cold." - Suzanne Millen

"There is something about the presence of a cat... that seems to take the bite out of being alone." - Louis J Camuti

"The real measure of a day's heat is the length of a sleeping cat." - Charles J Brady

"I collect records. And cats. I don't have any cats right now. But if I'm taking a walk and I see a cat, I'm happy." - Haruki Murakami

"While cats can be infuriating, little old women in fur coats, they make me laugh." - Rita Mae Brown

"I live alone, with cats, books, pictures, fresh vegetables to cook, the garden, the hens to feed." - Jeanette Winterson

"Puss on the hearth with velvet paws, sits wiping o'er his whiskered jaws." - Erasmus Darwin

"Even cats grow lonely and anxious." - Mason Cooley

"Outside, the north wind, coming and passing, swelling and dying, lifts the frozen sand drives it a-rattle against the lidless windows and we may dear sit stroking the cat stroking the cat and smiling sleepily, prrrr." - William Carlos Williams

"Books. Cats. Life is good." - Edward Gorey

"I take care of my flowers and my cats. And enjoy food. And that's living." - Ursula Andress

"Since each of us is blessed with only one life, why not live it with a cat?" - Robert Stearns

"Bless their little pointed faces and their big, loving, loyal hearts. If a cat did not put down a firm paw down now and then, how could his human remain possessed?" - Winifred Carriere

"Cats can be very funny, and have the oddest ways of showing they're glad to see you. Rudimac always peed in our shoes." - W H Auden

Here to sit by me, and turn
Glorious eyes that smile and burn,
Golden eyes, love's lustrous need,
On the golden page I read.

All your wondrous wealth of hair,
Dark and fair,
Silken-shaggy, soft and bright
As the clouds and beams of night,
Pays my reverent hand's caress
Back with friendlier gentleness." - Algernon Swinburne

"How many times have I rested tired eyes on her graceful little body, curled up in a ball and wrapped round with her tail like a parcel... if they are content, their contentment is absolute; and our jaded and wearied spirits find a natural relief in the sight of creatures whose little cups of happiness can so easily be filled to the brim." - Agnes Repplier

"Happiness does not light gently on my shoulder like a butterfly. She pounces on my lap, demanding that I scratch behind her ears." - Unknown

"Civilization is defined by the presence of cats." - Unknown

"He makes himself the companion of your hours of solitude, melancholy and toil. He remains for whole evenings on your knee, uttering his contented purr, happy to be with you, and forsaking the company of animals of his own species." - Theophile Gautier

"One may live in a house for six months with a cat and never receive from it a single kindly word or look... Yet, suddenly and without any cause, this very same cat will one day become, for half an hour or an hour, your dearest friend." - The Spectator, 26 February 1898

"We entertain a cat - he adorns our hearth as a guest, fellow-lodger and equal because he wishes to be there." - H P Lovecraft

"Most cats enjoy kneading - digging their claws into rugs, fabrics or human arms and legs. It exercises certain muscles, but I think they do it for fun, too." - Lloyd Alexander

"Me and the wife [singer Katy Perry] have three cats, and they get whatever they want. We can only know what they want from what we speculate, so it's a lot of vests, hats and cat shoes." - Russell Brand

"By associating with the cat, one only risks
becoming richer." - Colette

"Some of the best five minutes of my life have been spent sitting on garden walls sharing bags of popcorn with newly-made feline acquaintances." - Pam Brown

"One cat is fine. She will probably sleep over the hot water bottle, or in the crook of your knees or on your lap or folded in your arms, though there are eccentrics who prefer to wedge themselves under the chin, curl around the head, squat on the hip or ribcage or shoulders or simply insist on lying nose to nose, breathing kipper." - Rosemary Nisbet

"It is a well-known fact that the survival rate after heart-attacks is significantly higher among pet owners than non owners, and that human blood pressure falls in the presence of companion animals - especially cats." - Dr Maya Patel

"I wish you could see the two cats drowsing side by side in a Victorian nursing chair, their paws, their ears, their tails complementally adjusted, their blue eyes blinking open on a single thought of when I shall remember it's their suppertime. They might have been composed by Bach for two flutes." - Sylvia Townsend Warner

"Who needs television when you have cats?" - Lori Spigelmyer

"Cats may, indeed, be the thinking man's pet - because living with cats certainly keeps you on your toes!" - Barbara L Diamond

"There were pots of geraniums on the high window sill, with a tortoiseshell cat curled up between them where the sun made a splash. Cyril went across and stroked it - he was always fond of cats - and it got up, stretched itself, arched its back and purred. The clock ticked on slowly, and there was a faint buzzing of bees. It seemed as if nothing wanted to wake up." - Ernest H Shepard

"Frontin wasn't just a cat, he was a poodle for goodness, a camel for sobriety, a monkey for intelligence. In summer, he would follow me on walks through the woods at Romainville; in winter he never left my study. Curled up the whole day long on a cushion next to my desk, he would sleep as long as I worked, as if to avoid bothering me; but when I rose he would rise too, stretching his back and fixing me with his golden eyes as if to say , 'Now we can talk, right?' And we did." - Charles Paul De Kock

"Johnny has always felt that cockroaches make the best gifts. He gives them for every occasion." - Jane Denny, The Pride

"If your cat falls out of a tree, go indoors to laugh." - Patricia Hitchcock

"The cat cleans her face with a look of delight." -
John Clare

"We entertain a cat - he adorns our hearth as a guest, fellow-lodger and equal because he wishes to be there." - HP Lovecraft

"There is, indeed, no single quality of the cat that man could not emulate to his advantage." - Carl Van Vechten

"What greater gift than the love of a cat?" - Charles Dickens

"When you're special to a cat, you're special indeed... she brings to you the gift of her preference of you, the sight of you, the sound of your voice, the touch of your hand." - Leonore Fleisher

"If you are worthy of its affection, a cat will be your friend, but never your slave." - Theophile Gautier

"His friendship is not easily won but it is something worth having." - Michael Joseph

"One must love a cat on its own terms." - Paul Gray

"There is something about the presence of a cat... that seems to take the bite out of being alone." - Louis Camuti

"A cat does not want all the world to love her - only those she has chosen to love." - Helen Thomson

"I love in the cat that independent and most ungrateful temper which prevents it from attaching itself to anyone; the indifference with which it passes from the salon to the housetop." - Francois Rene De Chateaubriand

"There's nothing like the company of a cat. Your cat is a loyal friend, a warm sleeping-buddy, a playmate, a confidant, a presence... Cats bring joy and delight to everyday life. Stroking a cat can even lower your blood pressure." - Wendy Christensen

"The cat is for those who care little for demonstrative affection, and much more for the subtle intimacies of spirit." - Frank Swinnerton

"I don't understand people who don't touch their pets. Their cat or dog is called a pet for a reason." - Jarod Kintz

"There are only a few things that are more entertaining than watching a cat trying to run across a freshly waxed wood floor after a ball." - David C Holley, Write Like No One is Reading

"A fish tank is just interactive television for cats." - Oliver Gaspirtz, A Treasury of Pet Humor

"When bored, find a little cat and watch it; when very bored, find two little cats and watch them!" - Mehmet Murat Ildan

Cats Vs Dogs

"A dog will flatter you but you have to flatter the cat."- George Mikes

"The cat, which is a solitary beast, is single minded and goes its way alone; but the dog, like his master, is confused in his mind." - H G Wells

"I am fond of pigs. Dogs look up to us. Cats look down on us. Pigs treat us as equals." - Winston Churchill

"I love them, they are so nice and selfish. Dogs are TOO good and unselfish. They make me feel uncomfortable. But cats are gloriously human." - L M Montgomery, Anne of the Island

"You can keep a dog; but it is the cat who keeps people, because cats find humans useful domestic animals." - George Mikes

"Cats cooperate, dogs perform." - Brad Thompson

"A dog is like a liberal, he wants to please everybody. A cat doesn't really need to know that everybody loves him." - William Kunstler

"Even the stupidest cat seems to know more than any dog." - Eleanor Clark

"Dogs come when they're called. Cats take the message and call you back." - Mary Bly

"Every dog has his day - but nights belong to cats."
- Unknown

"I figured we all started out as cats, but then the world put us on a leash and collar and turned us into dogs." - Unknown

"With dogs and people, it's love in big splashy colors. When you're involved with a cat, you're dealing in pastels." - Louis Camuti

"If I prefer cats to dogs, this is because there is no police cat." - Jean Cocteau

"When choosing a pet, remember that a dog will consider you as his family, and a cat as a domestic." - Ron Dentinger

"Women and cats will do as they please, and men and dogs should relax and get used to the idea." - Robert A Heinlein

"If the dog embodies action, the cat is rather a symbol of reflection." - Marie-Luce Hubert

"A dog thinks: Hey, these people I live with feed me, love me, provide me with a nice warm, dry house, pet me, and take good care of me... They must be Gods! A cat thinks: Hey, these people I live with feed me, love me, provide me with a nice warm, dry house, pet me, and take good care of me... I must be a God!" - Ira Lewis

"The Cat's beauty is classical while the Dog's is gothic." - Howard Lovecraft

"A cat is rarely enthusiastic. A dog is, too often. A man, too." - Claude Roy

"Dogs eat. Cats dine." - Ann Taylor

"Apparently, the cat sees it as a point of honor to be of no use at all, this does not prevent him from claiming a better place at home than the dog." - Michel Tournier

"If animals could speak the dog would be a blundering outspoken fellow, but the cat would have the rare grace of never saying a word too many." - Mark Twain

"Cats are smarter than dogs. You cannot get eight cats to pull a sled through snow." - Jeff Valdez

"Cats are cleverer than dogs. Throw a ball for a cat and she'll expect you to have it biked back." - Jasmine Birtles

"Cats don't bark and act brave when they see something small in fur or feathers, they kill it. Dogs tend to bravado. They're braggarts. In the great evolutionary drama the dog is Sergeant Bilko, the cat is Rambo." - James Gorman

"With dogs and people, it's love in big splashy colors. When you're involved with a cat, you're dealing in pastels." - Louis A Camuti

"Artists like cats; soldiers like dogs." - Desmond
Morris

"Cats are the ultimate narcissists. You can tell this because of all the time they spend on personal grooming. Dogs aren't like this. A dog's idea of personal grooming is to roll on a dead fish." - James Gorman

"I used to love dogs until I discovered cats." - Nafisa Joseph

"Dogs have important jobs, like barking when the doorbell rings, but cats have no function in a house whatsoever." - W. Bruce Cameron, A Dog's Purpose

"Owners of dogs will have noticed that, if you provide them with food and water and shelter and affection, they will think you are god. Whereas owners of cats are compelled to realize that, if you provide them with food and water and shelter and affection, they draw the conclusion that they are gods." - Christopher Hitchens, The Portable Atheist: Essential Readings for the Nonbeliever

"Dogs are farmers and farmers' animals, cats are gentlemen and gentlemen's animals." - Howard P Lovecraft

"Dogs believe they are human. Cats believe they are God." - Jeff Valdez

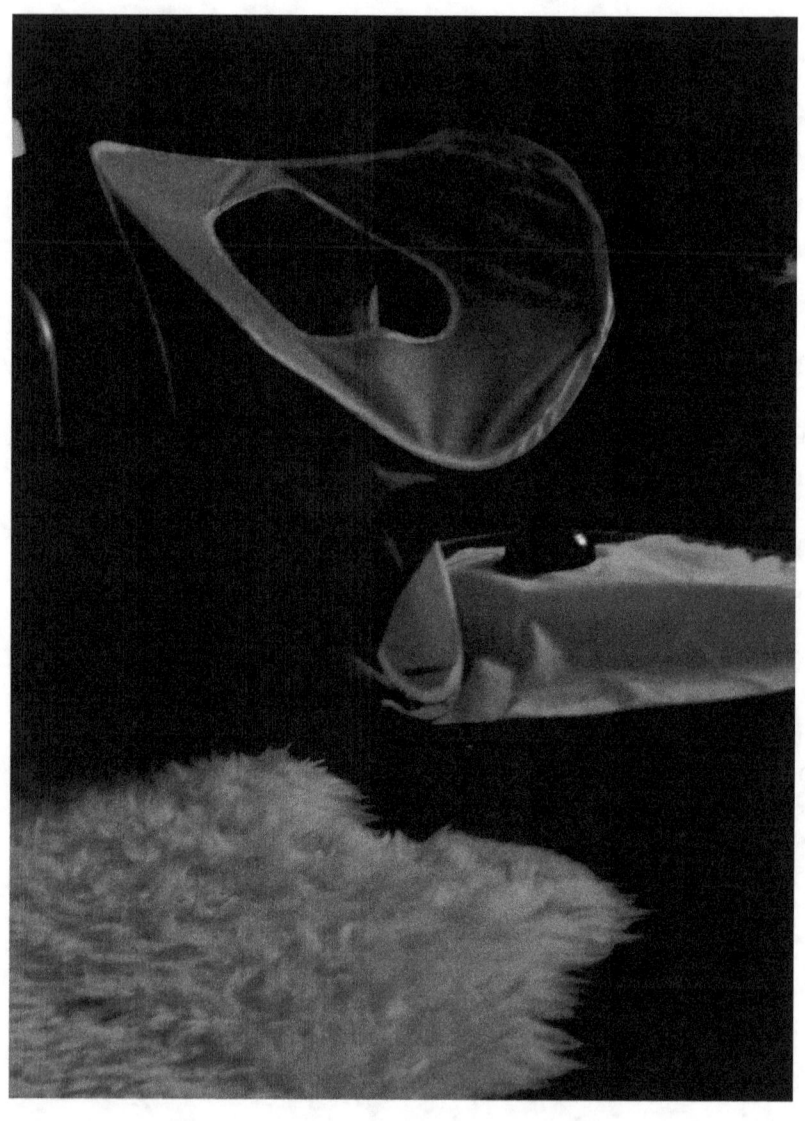

"Dogs have owners, cats have staff." - Unknown

"If dogs are like high school, cats are like a really tough Ph.D. program." - Siobhan Adcock, 30 Things Everyone Should Know How to Do Before Turning 30

"One feels so immensely flattered when chosen by a discriminating cat, for it is an affection which can only be won by merit, and never bought. A dog will love any wreck of humanity who chances to own him, but one needs to be self-respecting to earn the love of a cat. Pussies show their regard in such dignified little ways. When you open the hall door your cat will come half way down stairs to meet you, and will then turn and walk up before you with tail erect, and you feel as heartily welcome as though a dog had jumped all over you and knocked your hat off in the exuberance of his greeting. You notice cats never follow, never even walk by your side-they precede by a sort of divine right." - Kate A Hall, Cat Farming in California

"Men prefer pets they can control, like dogs. They can't handle that "get stuffed" stare from a cat." - Celia Hammond, Evening Standard Magazine, Mar. 26, 1999

"Dogs believe every stranger is a friend they haven't met yet. Cats wait for a proper invitation." - Vicki Brown

"Dogs have their day but cats have 365." - Lilian Jackson Braun

"Throw a stick, and the servile dog wheezes and pants and stumbles to bring it to you. Do the same before a cat, and he will eye you with coolly polite and somewhat bored amusement. And just as inferior people prefer the inferior animal which scampers excitedly because someone else wants something, so do superior people respect the superior animal which lives its own life and knows that the puerile stick-throwings of alien bipeds are none of its business and beneath its notice. The dog barks and begs and tumbles to amuse you when you crack the whip. That pleases a meekness-loving peasant who relishes a stimulus to his self importance. The cat, on the other hand, charms you into playing for its benefit when it wishes to be amused; making you rush about the room with a paper on a string when it feels like exercise, but refusing all your attempts to make it play when it is not in the humour. That is personality and individuality and self-respect - the calm mastery of a being whose life is its own and not yours - and the superior person recognises and appreciates this because he too is a free soul whose position is assured, and whose only law is his own heritage and aesthetic sense." - H P Lovecraft

"If you make a fool of yourself in front of a cat, he will sneer at you, if you are sober; he will leave the room if you are drunk. If you make a fool of yourself in front a dog, he will make a fool of himself, too." - Chuck Jones

"Your cat will never threaten your popularity by barking at three in the morning. He won't attack the mailman or eat the drapes, although he may climb the drapes to see how the room looks from the ceiling." - Helen Powers

"Cats will outsmart dogs every time." - John Grogan

"It took a thousand years to domesticate the dog. Cats took far less time to domesticate the human." - Lyn McConchie

"'And how do you know that you're mad?' 'To begin with,' said the Cat, 'a dog's not mad. You grant that?' 'I suppose so', said Alice. 'Well then,' the Cat went on, 'you see a dog growls when it's angry, and wags its tail when it's pleased. Now I growl when I'm pleased, and wag my tail when I'm angry. Therefore I'm mad.'" - Lewis Carroll, Alice's Adventures in Wonderland & Through the Looking-Glass

"Once when I had remarked on the affection quite often found between cat and dog, my friend replied, 'Yes. But I bet no dog would ever confess it to the other dogs.'" - C S Lewis, The Four Loves

"When someone asks, Dogs or cats? I usually say, For what, dinner?" - Jarod Kintz, This is the best book I've ever written, and it still sucks

"Dogs own space and cats own time." - Nicola
Griffith, Hild

"You know how cats do. They hide to die. Dogs come home." - Thomas Harris, Red Dragon

"Cats are very independent animals. They're very sexy, if you want. Dogs are different. They're familiar. They're obedient. You call a cat, you go, 'Cat, come here.' He doesn't come to you unless you have something in your hand that he thinks might be food. They're very free animals, and I like that." - Antonio Banderas

"You own a dog but you feed a cat." - Jenny de Vries

"Cats are poetry in motion; dogs are gibberish in neutral." - Anonymous

"Your cat will never threaten your popularity by barking at three in the morning. He won't attack the mailman or eat the drapes, although he may climb the drapes to see how the room looks from the ceiling." - Helen Powers

"Cats are to dogs what modern people are to the people we used to have. Cats are slimmer, cleaner, more attractive, disloyal, and lazy. It's easy to understand why the cat has eclipsed the dog as modern America's favorite pet. People like pets to possess the same qualities they do. Cats are irresponsible and recognize no authority, yet are completely dependent on others for their material needs. Cats cannot be made to do anything useful.

Cats are mean for the fun of it. In fact, cats possess so many of the same qualities as some people (expensive girlfriends, for instance) that it's often hard to tell the people and the cats apart." - P J O'Rourke, Modern Manners

"If you throw a ball to a dog, he will run and catch it. But this is not what a cat will do." - Jim Davis (Garfield)

"What do we get if we remove half the brain of a cat? An intelligent dog!" - Jim Davis (Garfield)

"When choosing a pet, remember that a dog will consider you as his family, and a cat as a domestic." - Ron Dentinger

"The Cat's beauty is classical while the Dog's is gothic." - Howard Lovecraft

"Dogs are farmers and farmers' animals, cats are gentlemen and gentlemen's animals." - Howard P Lovecraft

"You can tell a dog to do something. You can put it to a cat as a reasonable proposition." - Michael Stevens

"You own a dog but you feed a cat." - Barbara Webster

"My cat brought me a toy. I thanked her and threw
it. She sat there gave me a look that made me

realize people and dogs are the crazy ones." - Dan Harmon

"Dogs are exceptionally intelligent creatures. My dog, for example, taught me that not only am I a cat person, but that it isn't really a dog at all, but that it is in fact a cat." - Jarod Kintz, This is the best book I've ever written, and it still sucks

"We get a lot of calls where the person is murdered at home, but is not found for a period of time. And so the animals have already started to take the body apart because they haven't been fed in that period. So your evidence is being chewed up by the family pet.

I tell you - Dogs are more loyal than cats. Cats will wait only a certain period of time and they'll start chewing on you. Dogs will wait a day or two before they just can't take the starving anymore. So, keep that in mind when choosing a pet.

You know how a cat just stares at you, maybe at the top of the TV, from across the room? That's because they're watching to see if you're gonna stop breathing." - Connie Fletcher, Every Contact Leaves a Trace

"'You know what I should do?' Hoshino asked, excited. 'Of course,' the cat said. 'What'd I tell you? Cats know everything. Not like dogs.' - Haruki Murakami, Kafka on the Shore

"Dogs have hair. Cats, fur.
Dogs whine, yip, howl, bark. Cats purrr.
I say: No contest." - Lee Wardlaw, Won-Ton: A Cat
Tale Told in Haiku

"Cats have the curiosity of a genius, while dogs
have the intellect of a sack of manure covered in
hair and mulch made from bark (so loud). Actually,
that assessment isn't quite fair. Sacks of manure are
smarter than dogs, and make better best friends (I
should know, because I've lost three best friends to
landscaping incidents in the last year alone, which
left me alone)." - Jarod Kintz, At even one penny,
this book would be overpriced. In fact, free is too
expensive, because you'd still waste time by reading
it.

"The dog appeals to cheap and facile emotions; the
cat to the deepest founts of imagination and cosmic
perception in the human mind. It is no accident that
the contemplative Egyptians, together with such
later poetic spirits as Poe, Gautier, Baudelaire, and
Swinburne, were all sincere worshippers of the
supple grimalkin." - H P Lovecraft, Cats and Dogs

"One of the good things about cats is that, unlike
dogs, they don't come up to you in the street and try
to have sex with your leg." - Tom Cox, The Good,
the Bad and the Furry: Life with the World's Most
Melancholy Cat and Other Whiskery Friends

"Dogs are like kids. Cats are like roommates." -
Oliver Gaspirtz, A Treasury of Pet Humor

"Dogs will give you unconditional love until the day they die. Cats will make you pay for every mistake you've ever made since the day you were born." - Oliver Gaspirtz, A Treasury of Pet Humor

"The cat is mighty dignified until the dog comes by." - Unknown

"It is easy to understand why the cat has eclipsed the dog as modern America's favorite pet. People like pets to possess the same qualities that they do. Cats are irresponsible and recognize no authority, yet are completely dependent on others for their material needs. Cats cannot be made to do anything useful. Cats are mean for the fun of it. In fact, cats possess so many of the same qualities as some people that it is often hard to tell people and cats apart." - P J O'Rourke

"The cat is a character of being, the dog is a character of doing." - Michael Rosen

"You need to get yourself a proper dog. Any dog under 50 pounds is a cat and cats are pointless" - Ron Swanson

"A dog is a man's best friend. A cat is a cat's best friend." - Robert J Vogel

"When you are a cat, you are a cat. When you are a cat you are not a dog." - Jacques Roubaud

"Your cat will never threaten your popularity by barking at three in the morning." - Helen Powers

"A dog is a pitiful thing, depending wholly on companionship, and utterly lost except in packs or by the side of his master. Leave him alone and he does not know what to do except bark and howl and trot about till sheer exhaustion forces him to sleep. A cat, however, is never without the potentialities of contentment. Like a superior man, he knows how to be alone and happy. Once he looks about and finds no one to amuse him, he settles down to the task of amusing himself; and no one really knows cats without having occasionally peeked stealthily at some lively and well-balanced kitten which believes itself to be alone." - H P Lovecraft, Cats and Dogs

"Why do I prefer cats to dogs? I have never stepped in cat shit." - Robert Black

"When the man was disgraced and told to go away, he was allowed to ask all the animals whether any of them would come with him and share his fortunes and his life. There were only two who agreed to come entirely of their own accord, and they were the dog and the cat. And ever since then, those two have been jealous of each other, and each is for ever trying to make man choose which one he likes best. Every man prefers one or the other." - Richard Adams, The Plague Dogs

"There are guide dogs but no guide cats." - Bernard Werber

"Apparently, the cat sees it as a point of honor to be of no use at all, this does not prevent him from claiming a better place at home than the dog." - Michel Tournier

"Who loves a cat loves all cats. Who loves his dog does not love the others." - Roland Topor

"It's funny how dogs and cats know the inside of folks better than other folks do, isn't it?" - Eleanor H Porter

"Any member introducing a dog into the Society's premises shall be liable to a fine of one pound. Any animal leading a blind person shall be deemed to be a cat." - Oxford Union Society

"I dressed my dog up as a cat for Halloween. Now he won't come when I call him." - Reid Faylor

"Dogs are eternally grateful that humans exist. Cats, however, are simply mildly appreciative." - Carl Brizzi

Cats and Writers

"Women, poets, and especially artists, like cats; delicate natures only can realize their sensitive systems." - Helen M Winslow

"Poets generally love cats - because poets have no delusions about their own superiority." - Marion Garretty

"Cats are dangerous companions for writers because cat watching is a near-perfect method of failing to write anything." - Dan Greenberg

"A catless writer is almost inconceivable. It's a perverse taste, really, since it would be easier to write with a herd of buffalo in the room than even one cat; they make nests in the notes and bite the end of the pen and walk on the typewriter keys." - Barbara Holland

"Perhaps it is because cats do not live by human patterns, do not fit themselves into prescribed behavior, that they are so united to creative people." - Andre Norton

"That's the great secret of creativity. You treat ideas like cats: you make them follow you." - Ray Bradbury, Zen in the Art of Writing

"For concentration you need a cat...And the tranquility of the cat will gradually come to affect you, sitting there at your desk, so that all the excitable qualities that impede your concentration compose themselves and give you back the self-command it has lost. You need not watch the cat all the time. Its presence is enough." - Muriel Spark

"A writer is never lonely with a cat." - Patricia Highsmith

"Authors like cats because they are such quiet, lovable, wise creatures, and cats like authors for the same reasons." - Robertson Davies

"That's the great secret of creativity. You treat ideas like cats: you make them follow you." - Ray Bradbury, Zen in the Art of Writing

"The poet is a man who lives at last by watching his moods. An old poet comes at last to watch his moods as narrowly as a cat does a mouse." - Henry David Thoreau

"Perhaps it is because cats do not live by human patterns, do not fit themselves into prescribed behavior, that they are so united to creative people." - Andre Norton

"Because of our willingness to accept cats as superhuman creatures, they are the ideal animals with which to work creatively." - Roni Schotter

"As an inspiration to the author, I do not think the cat can be over-estimated. He suggests so much grace, power, beauty, motion, mysticism. I do not wonder that many writers love cats; I am only surprised that all do not." - Carl Van Vechten

"If you want to be a psychological novelist and write about human beings, the best thing you can do is keep a pair of cats." - Aldous Huxley

"If by chance I seated myself to write, she very slyly, very tenderly, seeking protection and caresses, would softly take her place on my knee and follow the comings and goings of my pen -sometimes effacing, with an unintentional stroke of her paw, lines of whose tenor she disapproved." - Pierre Loti

"Cats offer writers something that humans cannot provide: a company that is neither protest nor disturbance and that is as soothing and changing as a very calm sea." - Patricia Highsmith

"Marco could not have known about the mystical effect of a full moon on cats and books left on their own in the library. Not until he saw the lines breathe, the words unveiled." - Rahma Krambo, Guardian Cats and the Lost Books of Alexandria

"Cats speak to poets in their natural tongue, and something profound and untamed in us answers." - Jean Burden

"If you want to write, keep cats." - Aldous Huxley

"When I am ready to work, the cat jumps off the desk and settles on my white sheet. You ask me how I can write? The fact is I write around the cat."
- Andre Malraux

"To Do Today, 1/17/08
1. Sit and think
2. Reach enlightenment
3. Feed the cats" - Jarod Kintz, I Should Have Renamed This

"I
think that the
world should be full of cats and full of rain, that's all, just
cats and
rain, rain and cats, very nice, good
night." - Charles Bukowski, Betting on the Muse: Poems and Stories

"And metaphors like cats behind your smile,
Each one wound up to purr,
each one a pride,
Each one a fine gold beast you've hid inside (...)" - Ray Bradbury, Zen in the Art of Writing

"If you're curious, you'll probably be a good journalist because we follow our curiosity like cats." - Diane Sawyer

"I wish I could write as mysterious as a cat." -
Edgar Allan Poe

"If you want to concentrate deeply on some problem, and especially some piece of writing or paper-work, you should acquire a cat. Alone with the cat in the room where you work... the cat will invariably get up on your desk and settle placidly under the desk lamp... The cat will settle down and be serene, with a serenity that passes all understanding. And the tranquility of the cat will gradually come to affect you, sitting there at your desk, so that all the excitable qualities that impede your concentration compose themselves and give your mind back the self-command it has lost. You need not watch the cat all the time. Its presence alone is enough. The effect of a cat on your concentration is remarkable, very mysterious." - Muriel Spark, A Far Cry from Kensington

"My writing, it's all I have. Well, aside from my health. And shelter, food, and clothing. Oh, and my cat." - Jarod Kintz, A Zebra is the Piano of the Animal Kingdom

"In fiction, I exercise my nosiness. I am as curious as my cats, and indeed that has led to trouble often enough and used up several of my nine lives. I am an avid listener. I am fascinated by other people's lives, the choices they make and how that works out through time, what they have done and left undone, what they tell me and what they keep secret and silent, what they lie about and what they confess, what they are proud of and what shames them, what they hope for and what they fear. The source of my fiction is the desire to understand people and their choices through time." - Marge Piercy, Braided Lives

"When I later discovered that she (illustrator Faith Jacques) was a compulsive reader who loved to be alone and kept cats because they are the only pets that allow you to be both, my adoration of Jacques and her work could only increase." - Lucy Mangan

"If you've got a cozy mystery, and a dog is introduced, readers' first question is, 'Does the dog die?' They never ask about a cat. They know that the first rule of cozies is: The Cat Never Dies." - K B Inglee, mystery writer

"If the cat takes possession of the sheet while his master is busy covering it with words, let the latter give in. This is a sign that what he had written wasn't worth much and that what was to come would have been worse." - Bernard Pivot

"A poet's cat, sedate and grave,
As poet well could wish to have,
Was much addicted to inquire
For nooks, to which she might retire,
And where, secure as mouse in chink,
She might repose, or sit and think.
I know not where she caught the trick -
Nature perhaps her self had cast her
In such a mode philosophique,
Or else she learn'd it of her master." - William Cowper

"They come to sit on the table by the writer, keeping his thoughts company, and gazing at him with intelligent tenderness and magical penetration. It seems as though cats divine the thought that is passing from the brain to the pen, and that as they stretch out a paw, they are trying to seize it on its way." - Theophile Gautier

Crazy Cat People

"There is, incidentally, no way of talking about cats that enables one to come off as a sane person." - Dan Greenberg

"If you can remember how many cats you have, you don't have enough." - Unknown

"Of course, maybe I'd end up like one of those crazy old people with, like, sixty cats. And one day, the neighbors would complain about the smell, and it would turn out I'd died and the cats had eaten me.

Still, it might be nice to have a cat." - Alex Flinn

"Some people own cats and go on leading normal lives." - Unknown

"You can tell your cat anything and he'll still love you. If you lose your job or your best friend, your cat will think no less of you." - Helen Powers

"People that don't like cats haven't met the right one yet." - Deborah A. Edwards

"People who love cats have some of the biggest hearts around." - Susan Easterly

"Two people meeting for the first time suddenly relax if they find they both have cats. And plunge into anecdote." - Charlotte Gray

"Cat lovers can readily be identified. Their clothes always look old and worn. Their sheets look like bath towels and their bath looks like a collection of knitting mistakes." - Eric Gurney

"One cat just leads to another." - Ernest Hemingway

"You can visualize a hundred cats. Beyond that, you can't. Two hundred, five hundred, it all looks the same." - Jack Wright

"For, though the room was silent, the silence of half a hundred cats is a peculiar thing, like fifty individual silences all piled one on top of another." - Susanna Clarke, Jonathan Strange and Mr Norrell

"I always thought I was going to end up an old spinster, with my cats and fur coats." - Gemma Arterton

"Cats are like potato chips - it's hard to have just one." - Sandra Charon, Planet Cat

"Cats are like shoes - you need them in a lot of colors." - Mari Skelly

"One day I was counting the cats and I absent-mindedly counted myself." - Bobbie Ann Mason, Shiloh and Other Stories

"The purity of a person's heart can be quickly measured by how they regard cats." - Unknown

"It is impossible for a lover of cats to banish these alert, gentle, and discriminating little friends, who give us just enough of their regard and complaisance to make us hunger for more." - Agnes Repplier

"Nobody who is not prepared to spoil cats will get from them the rewards that they are able to give to those who will spoil them." - Sir Compton Mackenzie

"There are several cats smoothly moving about, which helped me greatly to relax, for I have always felt that no house is wholly bad where there are cats, and conversely, where there are several cats, a house is bound to be wonderfully charming." - Hans Holzer, The Ghost Hunter

"'Cat rescue is like a virus,' says Des placidly about the cat obsession that has taken over his life. 'And once you're infected, it's incurable.'" - Denise Flaim, Rescue Ink: How Ten Guys Saved Countless Dogs and Cats, Twelve Horses, Five Pigs, One Duck, and a Few Turtles

"We need a country literally full of cat guys and cat girls, bikers, politicians, clergy, and everyone in between, in order to keep millions from dying without homes." - Jackson Galaxy

"Maybe this was why people filled their house with stinking cats, so they didn't notice that they were alone, so they wouldn't die without a living soul noticing." - Kate Atkinson, Case Histories

"If I tried to tell you how much I love my cats, you wouldn't believe me - unless your heart is also meow-shaped and covered in stray fur." - Lexie Saige, 2007

"Animal hoarding was a dirty secret until hoarders appeared on our TV screens and showed how they are compelled to collect so many dogs, cats or parrots that the animals end up in cages only inches bigger than their own bodies. For life." - Ingrid Newkirk

"I always had cats and animals, so children were never really in my thoughts." - Jacqueline Bisset

"I live for my cats. They are my only joy, my only pleasure in life. I do my utmost for them." - Agatha Christie

"...I regard cats as one of the great joys in the world. I see them as a gift of highest order." - Trisha McCagh

"I had at least a hundred cats, or rather, as Michelet said, a hundred cats got me." - Paul Morand

"Richelieu was not that unpleasant. He loved cats."
- Stephane Bern

"Cat people are different to the extent that they generally are non-conformists. How could they be otherwise with a cat running their lives?" - Louis Camuti

"Everyone on this planet loves cats. Whoever does not like them is an alien." - Jim Davis, Garfield

"People who love cats sometimes do have excessive confidence in intuition." - Annie Duperey

"People who love cats love their independence because this is what ensures their freedom." - Annie Duperey

"I've found that the way a person feels about cats-and the way they feel about him or her in return-is usually an excellent gauge by which to measure a person's character." - P C Cast, Marked

"I sometimes longed for someone who, like me, had not adjusted perfectly with his age, and such a person was hard to find; but I soon discovered cats, in which I could imagine a condition like mine, and books, where I found it quite often." - Julio Cortazar, Around the Day in Eighty Worlds

"I flung open the door. I got a momentary flash of about a hundred and fifteen cats of all sizes and colours scrapping in the middle of the room, and then they all shot past me with a rush and out of the front door; and all that was left of the mobscene was the head of a whacking big fish, lying on the carpet and staring up at me in a rather austere sort of way, as if it wanted a written explanation and apology." - P G Wodehouse, A Wodehouse Bestiary

"There should always be one more cat than person, so everyone has one to pet, and I have two to myself." - Jarod Kintz, This Book Title is Invisible

"There are several cats smoothly moving about, which helped me greatly to relax, for I have always felt that no house is wholly bad where there are cats, and conversely, where there are several cats, a house is bound to be wonderfully charming." - Hans Holzer, The Ghost Hunter

"It is a curious truth that many cats enjoy warmer, more convivial, even affectionate relationships with humans than they could ever do with fellow felines." - Bruce Fogle

"I don't understand people who don't touch their pets. Their cat or dog is called a pet for a reason." - Jarod Kintz, This Book is Not FOR SALE

"Cats are useless." - Mark Zupan

"Twenty-seven cats at one time hints at monomania, but in my case it was simpler. If you like cats and have some, you get kittens; and if you like kittens and enjoy having them about, they grow up and beget more cats for you." - Paul Gallico

"Boys annoyed her. Girls annoyed her. She should
have been a cat." - Katie Neipris

"I wish I had 15-20 cats that would serve as a blanket, like if I moved they would adjust to my new position, that would be good." - Megan Boyle

"I wish cats could float around your head." - Megan Boyle, Selected Unpublished Blog Posts of a Mexican Panda Express Employee

"I'm at a point in my life where I feel like I can't go anywhere. Maybe I'll try to coax my cat off my lap so I can get up and move." - Jarod Kintz, This is the best book I've ever written, and it still sucks

"If I were to show you pictures of my best friends, they'd all be cats." - Jarod Kintz, 99 Cents For Some Nonsense

"One of my biggest fears is that I'm going to die alone in my home, and my cats will eat me because I am too dead to open their food cans." - Kelli Jae Baeli, Bettered by a Dead Crustacean

"John and I noticed that whenever we talked about our children Wystan reached for his cats." - Thekla Clark

"He's better now, Loo. He's taking care of the cats." - C JoyBell C, Saint Paul Trois Chateaux: 1948

"My relationship with cats has saved me from a deadly, pervasive ignorance." - William S Burroughs, The Cat Inside

"A cat chooses its owner, not the other way around." - Helen Brown, Cleo

"Having a bunch of cats around is good. If you're feeling bad, you just look at the cats, you'll feel better, because they know that everything is, just as it is. There's nothing to get excited about. They just know. They're saviors. The more cats you have, the longer you live. If you have a hundred cats, you'll live ten times longer than if you have ten. Someday this will be discovered, and people will have a thousand cats and live forever. It's truly ridiculous." - Charles Bukowski, Interview Magazine, Sep. 1987

"Cat names give one a certain degree more confidence that the animal belongs to you." - Alan Ayckbourn

"I was only a small child when the seeds of cat enchantment were sown within me." - May Eustace

"The extraordinary thing about any cat is the effect it has on its owner." - Peter Gethers

"Everyone's pet is the most outstanding." - Jean Cocteau

"A cat's name may tell you more about its owners than it does about the cat." - Linda W Lewis

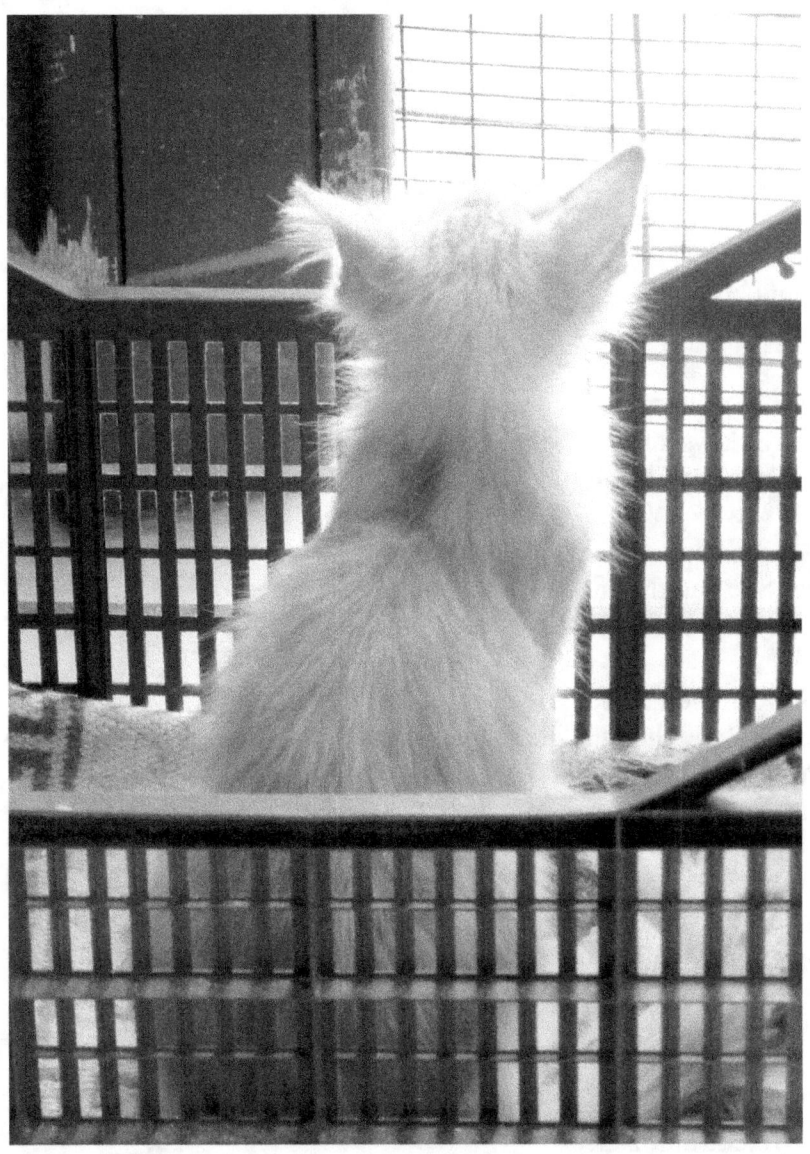

"She loves the smell of his fur, all warm and musky and cat-spit clean." - Sara Stark, An Untold Want

"Loving cats wasn't like loving skiing or comic books or arthouse films: when you walked into a pub, you usually didn't feel the need to tell people about it, either stylistically or verbally. I didn't try to hide the fact that I liked cats, it was just that a lot of the time it was hidden, by custom and by nature." - Tom Cox

"'Never believe a rumor of my death,' said Peter. 'I have as many lives as a cat. Also as many teeth, as many claws, and the same cheery, cooperative disposition.'" - Orson Scott Card, Xenocide

"She had other friends - friends that wouldn't leave her. She had the cats." - Jacqueline West, The Second Spy

"Sophie knew about power animals, everyone did...Sophie thought she might be a cat, she liked cats a lot." - Michelle Tea, Mermaid in Chelsea Creek

"Either you like cats or you don't. Whole nations have been divided on what people thought of an animal that mates openly, walks in silence and keeps its own counsel." - John Hillaby, Journey Through Europe

"I'm like a cat. I swear I have nine lives." - Jennifer L Armentrout, Deity

"When she bought the cats her mother asked her straight out if they were 'baby substitutes'. 'No,' Ruth had answered, straight-faced. 'They're kittens. If I had a baby it would be a cat substitute.'" - Elly Griffiths, The Crossing Places

"I'm a sucker for curiosity's whims. Does that make me a cat person?" - Richelle E Goodrich

"I would not have survived that dark time if it weren't for Cloudtail. He gave me another destiny, and I knew that no matter what I looked like, I would be all right. As long as Cloudtail loved me, I was no longer Lostface, but Brightheart." - Erin Hunter, Secrets of the Clans

"It is a truth universally acknowledged that a man in possession of a warm house and a well-stocked fridge must be in want of a cat." - Heather Hacking, How Cats Conquered the World

"There is no known cure for severe affection for one's cat. The only way to relieve the symptoms is to go ahead and launch a kiss attack." - Tichakorn Khroopan Hill

"Roen said, 'I can't quit. I have rent, and a cat to support.'" - Wesley Chu, The Lives of Tao

"I preferred to think of myself as a cat. If I think of my behavior as cat behavior instead of people behavior, it pretty much always makes sense." - Jael McHenry, The Kitchen Daughter

"'I didn't know you had a cat!' she exclaimed.

I am always surprised how many people make this observation-though not all are as bold as the American in giving voice to their astonishment. Why should His Holiness not have a cat-if indeed, 'having a cat' is a correct understanding of the relationship?" - David Michie, The Dalai Lama's Cat

"Cats choose us; we don't own them." - Kristin Cast

"I prefer cats to people, for the most part. Most people aren't cute, and if they are cute they rapidly outgrow it." - William S Burroughs

"The human race can be roughly divided into two categories: ailurophiles and ailurophobes - cat lovers and the underprivileged." - David Taylor, You and Your Cat

"So Nikki came aboard as Jaqueline's spare cat, presumably in case our prime cat, Eliza, goes on vacation, takes industrial action, or requests a personal day." - Christopher S Wren, The Cat Who Covered the World: The Adventures Of Henrietta And Her Foreign Correspondent

"Psychologists now recognize that the need in some people to have a dozen cats is really a sublimated desire to have two dozen cats." - Robert Brault, rbrault.blogspot.com

"Cat lovers can readily be identified. Their clothes always look old and well used. Their sheets look like bath towels and their bath towels look like a collection of knitting mistakes." - Eric Gurney

"When I first meet a cat, I want to pet them." - Jackson Galaxy

"We have three cats. It's like having children, but there's no tuition involved." - Ronald Reagan

"Never wear anything that panics the cat." - P J O'Rourke

"Maybe you can't change the whole world, but you can change the world for one cat." - Dusty Rainbolt

"My boyfriend said it was him or the cat...I miss him sometimes." - Unknown

"Other people's stories about their cats can be as tedious as stories about their children." - Sidney Denham

"Mad Cat Man is a less widely reported phenomenon than Mad Cat Lady, but I am here to tell you that he exists." - Tom Cox

"A house without a cat, how empty!" - Bertrand
Vac

"Loving cats is to be on the right side once and for all, it is abolishing the old superstitions, it is rehabilitating the heretics." - Louis Nucera

"My cat and I have an agreement: I leave her alone and don't make sudden moves when I wake up to find her perched on my chest, staring with an unblinking hostile gaze at my face and in return she rarely mutilates me." - James Nicoll

"I cannot deny that the cat lover and his cat have a master/slave relationship. The cat is the master." - Arthur R Kassin

"It isn't always easy being a father to a cat." - B L Diamond

"To some blind souls all cats are much alike. To a cat lover every cat from the beginning of time has been utterly and amazingly unique." - Jenny De Vries

"If you want to know the character of a man, find out what his cat thinks of him." - Unknown

"Nobody who is not prepared to spoil cats will get from them the reward they are able to give to those who do spoil them." - Compton MacKenzie

"The key to a successful new relationship between a cat and human is patience." - Susan Easterly

"People become fixated on cats. They turn into cat people. They think about their cats, talk obsessively about their cats, worry about their cats - and write about them." - Charles Elliott

"Cats are like potato chips - it's hard to have just one." - Sandra Charon

"Everyone who owns a cat is a cat-watcher." - Roger Caras

"I really am a cat transformed into a woman." - Brigitte Bardot

"It occurs to me that I can't remember ever reading about a murderer who gave house room to, or was fond of, a cat." - P D James

"GPS works great. I recommend it for all cat owners who want to know what their cats do when they're not there, if you can stand the ridicule from your friends." - Caroline Paul

"Tall, dark and handsome was hot. Tall, dark, and handsome with a nestled kitten? Atomic." - Chloe Neill

"I grew up with such an affinity to cats. I adore the way that they think and operate." - Guy Pearce

"I love my cats more than I love most people. Probably more than is healthy." - Amy Lee

"His attitude seemed to be, how can anyone not love a cat?" - Vicki Myron

"If I tried to tell you how much I love my cats, you wouldn't believe me." - Lexie Saige

"Getting a cat is a greater commitment than getting married." - Seymour Chwast and Paula Scher

"A cat chooses its owner, not the other way around." - Helen Brown

"The key to a successful new relationship between a cat and human is patience." - Susan Easterly

"The cat is the mirror of his human's mind." - Winifred Carriere

"Some people are born into cat-loving families, some achieve cats, and some have cats thrust upon them." - William H A Carr

"Cats are distant, discreet, impeccably clean and able to stay silent. What more could be needed to be good company?" - Marie Leczinska

"You can tell your cat anything and he'll still love you." - Helen Powers

"The difference between friends and pets is that friends we allow into our company, pets we allow into our solitude." - Robert Brault

Cat Haters

"Cat hate reflects an ugly, stupid, loutish, bigoted spirit." - William S Burroughs

"Cats are like insects. They should be left outside to clean up the garbage." - Michael Mewshaw, Playing Away

"Cats specialize in sneaky. Unpleasant creatures who think they own the world." - Emily Carmichael, Diamond in the Ruff

"Cats... have a natural affinity for people who don't like them - very perverse creatures." - Alan Goldsmith, Waldo Chicken Wakes the Dead

"Actually, I don't hate cats, I'm just kind of afraid of them." - Clay Aiken

"But cats to me are strange, so strange. I cannot sleep if one is near." - W H Davies

"Cats don't need to be possessed; they're evil on their own." - Peter Kreeft

"Rousseau pounced. Men who dislike cats were tyrannical: They do not like cats because the cat is free and will never consent to become a slave." - Robert Zaretsky, The Philosophers' Quarrel: Rousseau, Hume, and the Limits of Human Understanding

"Walter had never liked cats. They'd seemed to him the sociopaths of the pet world, a species domesticated as an evil necessary for the control of rodents and subsequently fetishized the way unhappy countries fetishize their militaries, saluting the uniforms of killers as cat owners stroke their animals' lovely fur and forgive their claws and fangs. He'd never seen anything in a cat's face but simpering incuriosity and self-interest; you only had to tease one with a mouse-toy to see where it's true heart lay...cats were all about using people." - Jonathan Franzen, Freedom

"Any conditioned cat-hater can be won over by any cat who chooses to make the effort." - Paul Corey

"By and large, people who enjoy teaching animals to roll over will find themselves happier with a dog." - Barbara Holland

"Don't want a cat
Scratching its claws all over my
Habitat
Giving no love and getting fat
Oh, you can get lonely
And a cat's no help with that." - Pet Shop Boys, I Want a DoG

"It's bad enough having dogs bring you bloody sticks all the time but a cat's idea of a present is a partially dismembered pigeon twitching on the lino. Well thanks a bunch Tiddles. I'll treasure it always."
- Craig Charles

"Cats are misunderstood, maligned, slandered by
ignorant people who thus often give the full

measure of their selfishness or wickedness." - Marcel Reney

"People that hate cats will come back as mice in their next life." - Faith Resnick

"I was drawn to his aloofness, the way cats gravitate toward people who'd rather avoid them." - Rachel Hartman, Seraphina

"I am not a cat man, but a dog man, and all felines can tell this at a glance - a sharp, vindictive glance." - James Thurber

"'I hated cats. I was a dog lover,' Des says with a shrug. 'What's the point of a cat? They're not affectionate. But that's because it's not my cat. I mean, your wife wouldn't jump on my lap. That's because she's your wife, not mine. Until you have your own cat, you really don't understand.'" - Denise Flaim, Rescue Ink: How Ten Guys Saved Countless Dogs and Cats, Twelve Horses, Five Pigs, One Duck, and a Few Turtles

"Sekhmet crawled onto Ramses's lap and began to purr. 'The creature oozes like a furry slug,' said Ramses, eyeing it without favor." - Elizabeth Peters, Seeing a Large Cat

"Walter had never liked cats. They'd seemed to him the sociopaths of the pet world, a species domesticated as an evil necessary for the control of rodents and subsequently fetishized the way unhappy countries fetishize their militaries, saluting the uniforms of killers as cat owners stroke their animals' lovely fur and forgive their claws and fangs. He'd never seen anything in a cat's face but simpering incuriosity and self-interest; you only had to tease one with a mouse-toy to see where it's true heart lay...cats were all about using people." - Jonathan Franzen, Freedom

"My cats inspire me daily. They inspire me to get a dog!" - Greg Curtis

"Very nice lady served us drinks in hotel and was followed in by a cat. We all crooned at it. Alan [Rickman] to cat (very low and meaning it): 'Fuck off.' The nice lady didn't turn a hair. The cat looked slightly embarrassed but stayed." - Emma Thompson, The Sense and Sensibility Screenplay and Diaries: Bringing Jane Austen's Novel to Film

"Cat hate reflects an ugly, stupid, loutish, bigoted spirit. There can be no compromise with this Ugly Spirit." - William S Burroughs, The Cat Inside

"Ever wonder why your cat jumps on the lap of the guest that doesn't like cats?

It is because people who don't like cats will do things cats like during greetings.

They squint their eyes, turn their heads and avoid direct contact with the cat. The cat's view is these people are saying hello and being non-threatening, and, sure enough, he ends up on their lap." - Carol Griglione, Animal Rescue League of Iowa for Love of Cats: A Hands on Journey

"It's like they've forgotten everything important, isn't it? I mean, forgotten things like cats and dancing exist." - Katherine Rundell

"All cats are possessed of a proud spirit, and the surest way to forfeit the esteem of a cat is to treat him as an inferior being." - Michael Joseph

"If you yell at a cat, you're the one who is making a fool of himself." - Unknown

They are full of fleas
And are smelly
However often you order
They do as they please." - Francois Coppee

"A cat is friendly in a hollow sort of way, like the way a prostitute is friendly." - Jonathan-David Jackson, The Quest for Juice

"The human race can be roughly divided into two categories: ailurophiles and ailurophobes - cat lovers and the underprivileged." - David Taylor, You and Your Cat

"Woman's knee, dog's nose, cat's paw: has there ever been anything so cold?" - Unknown

"If you hold a cat by the tail, you learn things you can't learn any other way." - Mark Twain

"The truth is that everybody loves animals but there are people who do not know that they love them. Can you imagine nature without animals, a prairie without insects, a forest without birds, mountains and plains without living beings? Imagine for a moment man alone and then what an immense desert, what silence, what stillness, what horrible sadness!" - Emile Zola

"If you shamefully misuse a cat once she will always maintain a dignified reserve toward you afterward. You will never get her full confidence again." - Mark Twain

"Cats are misunderstood, maligned, slandered by ignorant people who thus often give the full measure of their selfishness or wickedness." - Marcel Reney

"Mrs Crupp had indignantly assured him that there was not room to swing a cat there; but as Mr Dick justly observed to me, sitting down on the foot of the bed, nursing his leg, 'You know, Trotwood, I don't want to swing a cat. I never do swing a cat. Therefore what does that signify to me!'" - Charles Dickens

"When anyone mistreats it, the cat wants nothing more to do with that person and will remember him or her for a long time. It doesn't believe in the doctrine of turning the other cheek and won't pretend that it does." - Lawrence N Johnson

"Woman, cat and dog have fleas all along the year."
- Unknown

"'Mice, Kitchener, mice! Go seek!' cried my mother, who had no real vocation for cats." - Sylvia Townsend Warner

"Cats specialize in sneaky. Unpleasant creatures who think they own the world." - Emily Carmichael

Kittens, Kittens, Kittens

"It is a very inconvenient habit of kittens (Alice had once made the remark) that whatever you say to them, they always purr."- Lewis Carroll

"The kitten was six weeks old. It was enchanting, a delicate fairy-tale cat, whose Siamese genes showed in the shape of the face, ears, tail, and the subtle lines of its body. She sat, a tiny thing, in the middle of a yellow carpet, surrounded by five worshipppers, not at all afraid of us. Then she stalked around that floor of the house, inspecting every inch of it, climbed up on to my bed, crept under the fold of a sheet, and was at home." - Doris Lessing, On Cats

"The trouble with a kitten is THAT
Eventually it becomes a CAT." - Ogden Nash

"The kitten I got is black and white and has long hair. Really long hair (think Willie Nelson). I decided to call him Cap'n because his markings make him look like a pirate. The majority of his face is white, except over his left eye is a black patch of fur, like an eye patch, and under his chin he has black hair that's long and comes to a point like a goatee. Also, when I got him he had a parrot on his shoulder and a wooden leg." - Jarod Kintz, Gosh

"There is no more intrepid explorer than a kitten." - Jules Champfleury

"One day on opening the shutters of your house, intrigued by cries you hear deep in your garden, you go out to find the origin of them and there under the pile of wood, you are face to face with a small frightened hairball : a kitten." - Pierre-Yves Dumoulin

"The playful kitten with its pretty little tigerish gambol is infinitely more amusing than half the people one is obliged to live with in the world." - Lady Sydney Morgan

"A kitten is chiefly remarkable for rushing about like mad at nothing whatever, and generally stopping before it gets there." - Agnes Repplier

"A kitten is the most irresistible comedian in the world. Its wide-open eyes gleam with wonder and mirth. It darts madly at nothing at all, and then, as though suddenly checked in the pursuit, prances sideways on its hind legs with ridiculous agility and zeal." - Agnes Repplier

"Confront a child, a puppy, and a kitten with a sudden danger; the child will turn instinctively for assistance, the puppy will grovel in abject submission, the kitten will brace its tiny body for frantic resistance." - Saki

"Even a kitten would not believe such stupidities." - Joann Sfar, the Rabbi's Cat

"An ordinary kitten will ask more questions than any five-year old." - Carl Van Vechten

"Kittens are born with their eyes shut. They open them in about six days, take a look around, then close them again for the better part of their lives." - Stephen Baker

"He raised his head and emitted an impressive yowl for a creature only four inches in length, tip-to-tail." - Patricia Khuly

"A kitten...does not discover that her tail belongs to her until you tread on it." - Henry David Thoreau

"The kitten has a luxurious, Bohemian, unpuritanical nature. It eats six meals a day, plays furiously with a toy mouse and a piece of rope, and suddenly falls into a deep sleep whenever the fit takes it. It never feels the necessity to do anything to justify its existence; it does not want to be a Good Citizen; it has never heard of Service. It knows that it is beautiful and delightful, and it considers that a sufficient contribution to the general good. And in return for its beauty and charm it expects fish, meat, and vegetables, a comfortable bed, a chair by the grate fire, and endless petting." - Robertson Davies, The Diary of Samuel Marchbanks

"Take care of my babies. Take them with you wherever you go." - William S Burroughs, The Cat Inside

"Kittens believe that all nature is occupied with their diversion." - F A Paradis de Moncrief

"A kitten is the delight of a household. All day long a comedy is played out by an incomparable actor." - Jules Champfleury

"A kitten is so flexible that she is almost double; the hind parts are equivalent to another kitten with which the forepart plays. She does not discover that her tail belongs to her until you tread on it."- Henry David Thoreau

"Kitten, my kitten, soft and dear,
I am so glad that we are here
Sitting together just us two,
You loving me and me loving you." - Marchette Chute, My Kitten

"It is impossible to keep a straight face in the presence of one or more kittens." - Cynthia E Varnado

"I named my kitten Rose - fur soft as a petal, claws sharper than thorns." - Astrid Alauda

"A kitten is, in the animal world, what a rosebud is in the garden." - Robert Southey

"Never pick up a stray kitten... unless you've already made up your mind to be owned by it." - Robert A Heinlein

"All kittens are cute until they grow up and become ugly." - Jim Davis, Garfield

"The smallest kitten only needs a week to be in full possession of a house and its owners." - Pam Brown

"All kittens, from the very first, set out to teach their humans to adapt to the needs of a cat. As a reward, they grant them the position of honorary cat." - Pam Brown

"Kittens learn early to listen intently when someone calls them - and do absolutely nothing." - Pam Brown

"A pear shaped kitten hanging by his front claws is in trouble and should be unhooked at once. From apple trees, pelmets and loft ladders. He should not be told he's an idiot. His pride is hurt enough." - Pam Brown

"I hope people don't take kittens on a whim, like they would a toy, then not care for them." - Shirley Rousseau Murphy, Cat on the Money

"May 4, 1985. I am packing for a short trip to New York to discuss the cat book with Brion. In the front room where the kittens are kept, Calico Jane is nursing one black kitten. I pick up my Tourister. It seems heavy. I look inside and there are her other four kittens.

"Caldris led them over to a large covered basket that sat on the stones near the docked dinghy. He undid the cover, reached in and removed a live kitten. 'Hello, you monstrous little necessity'. 'Mrrrrwwwwww', said the monstrous little necessity." - Scott Lynch, Red Seas Under Red Skies

"Some of them stole off to those cryptical realms which are known only to cats and which villagers say are on the moon's dark side, whither the cats leap from tall housetops; but one small black kitten crept upstairs and sprang in Carter's lap to purr and play, and curled up near his feet when he lay down at last on the little couch whose pillows were stuffed with fragrant drowsy herbs." - H P Lovecraft, The Dream-Quest of Unknown Kadath

"'Opinions are like kittens,' he commented. 'People are always giving them away.'" - Elizabeth Bear, Ad Eternum

"Kittens are angels with whiskers." - Alexis Flora Hope

"Kittens can happen to anyone." - Paul Gallico

"If he is comic, it is only because of the incongruity of so demure a look and so wild a heart." - Alan Devoe

"Do you see that kitten chasing so prettily her own tail? If you could look with her eyes, you might see her surrounded with hundreds of figures performing complex dramas, with tragic and comic issues, long conversations, many characters, many ups and downs of fate." - Ralph Waldo Emerson

"Caresses never turned a tiger into a kitten." -
Franklin Delano Roosevelt

"You may...if you try hard enough, be able to enter into a very small part of a cat's world...But the world of a kitten is almost impenetrable and you must rest content, mostly, to play the role of spectator. Unless you are tragically handicapped by the lack of any sense of humour you should be able to enjoy yourself." - Philip Brown

"Kittens are wide-eyed, soft and sweet. With needles in their jaws and feet." - Pam Brown

"A mother cat warns her kittens of danger by growling at them and the kittens know what she means. A mother cat warns off another cat or dog by growling and the kittens know what she means. A mother cat warns the kittens off her own food by growling and they know what she means. These growls sound all the same to humans, but not, evidently, to cats." - Peter Gray

"A kitten can
Bite with his feet;
Papa and Mamma
Have more teeth." - Theodore Roethke

"One dry slim paw, like that of a black rabbit, threatened the heavens; and a tiny kitten spotted like a civet cat, slumbering replete and prostrate on its back in the middle of this disorder, looked as though it had been assassinated..." - Colette

"I have just been given a very engaging Persian kitten... and his opinion is that I have been given to him." - Evelyn Underhill

"Even a kitten would not believe such stupidities." - Joann Sfar, the Rabbi's Cat

"A beating heart and an angel's soul, covered in fur." - Lexie Saige

"The kitten went, or rather hopped, down the stairs, each of which was twice her height: first front paws, then flop with the back; front paws, then flop with the back." - Doris Lessing

"If there is one thing this town has plenty of, it is kittens, which finally grow up to be cats, and go snooping around ash cans, and mer-owning on roofs, and keeping people from sleeping good." - Damon Runyon

"Domesticated felines remain 'part-kitten' all through their lives, and even though they may be middle-aged in feline terms they still look upon their human owners as their mothers." - Desmond Morris

"The cat carelessly carries the kitten by the scruff of the neck. As a package." - Michel Tournier

Old Cats

"Nothing's more playful than a young cat, nor more grave than an old one." - Thomas Fuller

"Cats were the gangsters of the animal world, living outside the law and often dying there. There were a great many of them who never grew old by the fire." - Stephen King, Pet Sematary

"If only cats grew into kittens." - R D Stern

"Arise from sleep, old cat,
And with great yawns and stretchings...
Amble out for love" - Issa, Japanese Haiku: Two Hundred Twenty Examples of Seventeen-Syllable Poems

"I shall never forget the indulgence with which he treated Hodge, his cat, for whom he used to go out and buy oysters, lest the servants having that trouble should take a dislike to the poor creature... I recollect him one day scrambling up on Dr. Johnson's breast, apparently with much satisfaction while my friend, smiling and half-whistling, rubbed his back and pulled him by the tail; and when I observed he was a fine cat, saying, 'Why, yes, Sir, but I have had cats whom I liked better than this,' And then as if perceiving Hodge to be out of countenance, adding, 'But he is a very fine cat, a very fine cat indeed.'" - James Boswell

"He was massive, a veritable Arnold Schwarzenegger of a cat, with a wide, handsome face and a proud, lionish expression." - Nicholas Dodman

"Pluto was a well-known fixture in Bad Munstereifel, at least among those who lived in the old part of town. A large, foul-tempered, and unsterilized inky-black tomcat, he had once made it onto the front page of the local free paper (admittedly during a quiet week as regards other news) after a resident of the town accused him of making an unprovoked attack on her pet dachshund." - Helen Grant, The Vanishing of Katharina Linden

"One was an ancient tortoiseshell cat with arthritis, who creaked around the house - but when Aunt Sibby flickered her fingers and crooned, Miminy, miminy, tall-as-a-chi-mi-ny, danced on his hind legs like a kitten." - Jane Louise Curry, Parsley Sage, Rosemary & Time

"She is a sprightly cat, hardly past her youth...she darts out a paw, and begins plucking it and inquiring into the matter, as if it were a challenge to play, or something lively enough to be eaten. What a graceful action of that foot of hers, between delicacy and petulance! - combining something of a thrust out, a beat and a scratch." - Leigh Hunt

"I called my cat William because no shorter name fits the dignity of his character. Poor old man, he has fits now, so I call him Fitz-William." - Josh Billings

"A grey old cat his whiskers licked beside;

A type of sadness in the house of pride." - George Crabbe

"Gentlemen, I used to have a cat here, by the name of Tom Quartz, which you'd a took an interest in I reckon-most any body would. I had him here eight year-and he was the remarkablest cat I ever see. He was a large gray one of the
Tom specie, an' he had more hard, natchral sense than any man in this camp-'n' a power of dignity-he wouldn't let the Gov'ner of Californy be familiar with him. He never ketched a rat in his life-'peared to be above it." - Mark Twain

"Polly-Hodge still purrs, still grooms herself fastidiously and obviously still enjoys life. When the moment comes when that life is no longer agreeable and it is apparent that she is suffering it will be painlessly ended. We are often more merciful to our animals than we are to each other." - P D James

"Here is an old cat who does not play, doesn't arch his back anymore and runs away whenever he sees a child; this is experience." - Edmond and Jules de Goncourt

"Cats have a sense of humour, as is shown in their extreme love of play. A middle-aged cat will often play as unreservedly as a kitten, though he knows perfectly well it is only a game." - William Lyon Phelps

"Alas old animals are so much nicer; I love my cat now, but it took about 8 years." - Nancy Mitford

After Cats Have Gone

"When you're used to hearing purring
and suddenly it's gone,
it's hard to silence the blaring sound of sadness." -
Missy Altijd

"For every house is incomplete without him, and a
blessing is lacking in the spirit." - Christopher
Smart

"Heaven would not heaven be, without my cats to
welcome me." - Unknown

"When Zoe died, it was really easy to explain to
people how much you could miss a sweet, gentle cat
who was nothing but a ball of utter love. I'm going
to have a much harder time one day, months or even
years from now, explaining why I miss the meanest,
grumpiest and most dangerous cat I've ever
encountered." - Neil Gaiman

"I believe cats to be spirits come to earth. A cat, I
am sure, could walk on a cloud without coming
through." - Jules Verne

"No amount of time can erase the memory of a
good cat, and no amount of masking tape can ever
totally remove his fur from your couch." - Leo
Dworken

"Cats come and go without ever leaving." - Martha
Curtis

"To all cats who left for "I don't know what heaven"
Hoping to see them again one day." - Joelle Dutillet

"I thought of Bobby, of the last look he had given
me, and at that moment I understood one of the
differences between man and cat: man knows he's
going to die, so he can get ready and be willing,
even eager, to go. A cat knows the end is near, but
that's all. He can't accept death: he can't trust in it;
cats are perhaps too metaphysical an entity to need
to believe in the idea of a beyond; a cat is his own
god and man his creation." - Jaime Manrique

"Another cat? Perhaps. For love there is also a
season; its seeds must be re-sown. But a family cat
is not replaceable like a worn-out coat or a set of
tires. Each new kitten becomes its own cat, and
none is repeated. I am four cats old, measuring out
my life in friends that have succeeded but not
replaced one another." - Irving Townsend

"I sometimes think the Pussy-Willows grey
Are Angel Kittens who have lost their way,
And every Bulrush on the river bank
A Cat-Tail from some lovely Cat astray." - Oliver
Herford, The Rubaiyat of a Persian Kitten

"I want to tell you that one of the cruelest hours,
amid the dreadful hours I've spent, was when I
learned the sudden death away from me, of the
faithful little companion, who for nine years had
never left me." - Emile Zola

"Housemate, I can think you still
Bounding to the window-sill
Over which I vaguely see
Your small mound beneath the tree,
Showing in the Autumn shade
That you moulder where you played." - Thomas
Hardy

"My cat is dead
But I have decided not to make a big tragedy out
Of it." - Wendy Cope

"Anyone who has owned many cats in long
succession can define his or her life as a series of
furry episodes." - Roger Caras

"The one disservice animals render us is that they
don't live as long as we do. But cats live longer than
dogs." - Doreen Tovey

"My old black cat, he passed away this morning. He
never knew what a heartache was. Woke up late and
he danced till noon. If questioned why, answered
just because. He never spoke much, preferring
silence. Eight lost lives was all he had." - Ian
Anderson

Bedtime...or not

"The trouble with sharing one's bed with cats is that they'd rather sleep on you than beside you." - Pam Brown

"A cat allows you to sleep on the bed. On the edge." - Jenny de Vries

"When dogs leap onto your bed, it's because they adore being with you. When cats leap onto your bed, it's because they adore your bed." - Alisha Everett

"Most beds sleep up to six cats. Ten cats without the owner." - Stephen Baker

"Sleeping together is a euphemism for people, but tantamount to marriage with cats." - Marge Percy

"I don't mind a cat, in its place. But its place is not right in the middle of my back at 4am." - Maynard Good Stoddard

"Cats are rather delicate creatures and they are subject to a lot of ailments, but I never heard of one who suffered from insomnia." - Joseph Wood Krutch

"Apparently, through scientific research, it has been determined that a cat's affection gland is stimulated by snoring, thus explaining my cat's uncontrollable urge to rub against my face at 2 am." - Terri L Haney

"A sleeping cat is ever alert." - Fred Schwab

"Because his long, white whiskers tickled, I began every day laughing." - Janet F Faure

"The best kind of alarm clock is the purring kind." - Terri Guillemets

"It's 8am and time to rest
It's 10am and time to relax
It's noon and time for repose
It's 3pm and time for shut-eye
It's 6pm and time for siesta
It's 9pm and time to slumber
It's midnight and time to snooze
It's 4am and time to hang upside down from your bedroom ceiling, screaming." - Francesco Marciuliano

"In my experience, cats and beds seem to be a natural combination." - Louis J Camuti

"Cats do care. For example, they know instinctively what time we have to be at work in the morning and they wake us up twenty minutes before the alarm goes off." - Michael Nelson

"A cat is convinced that it can wake you without actually disturbing you - by licking your eyelids gently, - by prizing them open with careful claws, - or by ramming its foot up your nose." - Pam Brown

"Behold the day-break!
I awaken you by sitting on your chest and purring in your face,
I stir you with muscular paw-prods, I rouse you with toe-bites,
Walt, you have slept enough, why don't you get up?" - Henry N Beard, Poetry for Cats: The Definitive Anthology of Distinguished Feline Verse

"In the morning, when she wishes me to wake, she crouches on my chest, and pats my face with her paw. Or, if I am on my side, she crouches looking into my face. Soft, soft touches of her paw. I open my eyes, say I don't want to wake. I close my eyes. Cat gently pats my eyelids. Cat licks my nose. Cat starts purring, two inches from my face. Cat, then, as I lie pretending to be asleep, delicately bites my nose. I laugh and sit up. At which she bounds off my bed and streaks downstairs - to have the back door opened if it is winter, to be fed, if it is summer." - Doris Lessing, On Cats

"Mimi slept not only indoors, but in Father Adams's armchair, on his corduroy waistcoat which he took off specially for her each night before he went to bed." - Doreen Tovey

"Sometimes he curls up on my pillow during the night and I don't know he's there until I yawn and my mouth closes on a whisker." - Astrid Alauda

"Many a cat can only be lured in by switching off all the lights and keeping very still. Until the indignant cry of a cat-locked-out comes at the door." - Pam Brown

"You are asleep. Deep, deep asleep - and then the world caves in. The cat has leapt from the top window to your stomach. He is saturated. He is hungry. He taps you into full wakefulness with a sodden paw. 'Could you open a can?'" - Pam Brown

"Cats don't mind sharing the bed with fellow cats, as long as the area is equitably divided among them. Usually there is room for everyone on a first-come first-served basis - under the blanket, on top of the blanket, on the pillow, under the pillow, at the head of the bed, at the foot of the bed, in that order. Any space left goes to the owner." - Stephen Baker

"Cats mewed angrily, vaulted their soft back whose hair bristled, straightened their tail and looked at him with eyes that glowed in the night." - Paul Sebillot

"Hawks for sunlight; owls half-light; but for the night, cats." - Doris Lessing

"It's always blackest just before you step on the cat." - Unknown

"I don't know he's there until I yawn and my mouth closes on a whisker." - Astrid Alauda

"If he is asleep in the middle of the bed when it's time for my day to end, I sleep curled up in a corner of the mattress." - Peter Gethers

"I wake up
to my cats
judging me.
They stare
blankly
as if to say,
'Is this what
you had in mind
for your life?
If it is, you may
want to consider
sleeping pills or
a tall bridge
because in our view,
you're pathetic.'

Or

they're hungry." - Pamela August Russell, B Is for Bad Poetry

"Sleep is like a cat: It only comes to you if you ignore it. I drank more and continued my mantra. 'Stop thinking', swig, 'empty your head', swig, 'now, seriously empty your head'." - Gillian Flynn, Gone Girl

"Cities, like cats, will reveal themselves at night." - Rupert Brooke

"When all candles be out, all cats be gray." - John Heywood

"We shall see that at which dogs howl in the dark, and that at which cats prick up their ears after midnight." - H P Lovecraft

"The cat has always been associated with the moon. Like the moon it comes to life at night, escaping from humanity and wandering over housetops with its eyes beaming out through the darkness." - Patricia Dale-Green

"A black cat dropped soundlessly from a high wall, like a spoonful of dark treacle, and melted under a gate." - Elizabeth Lemarchand

"...when I returned home at night, he was pretty sure to be waiting for me near the gate, and would rise and saunter along the walk, as if his being there was purely accidental..." - Charles Dudley Warner

"A black cat among roses,
phlox, lilac-misted under a quarter moon,
the sweet smells of heliotrope and night-scented
stock. The garden is very still.
It is dazed with moonlight,
contented with perfume..." - Amy Lowell

"It is said: at night all cats are gray. False: at night,
all cats are sleeping." - Patrick Timsit

"Minnaloushe creeps through the grass
Alone, important and wise,
And lifts to the changing moon
His changing eyes." - W B Yeats

"But cats to me are strange, so strange!
I cannot sleep if one is near;
And though I'm sure I see those eyes,
I'm not so sure a body's there!" - W H Davies

Catnip

"There's no thrilling anticipation of the day's first cup of coffee... nor the eye-closing delight of that first swallow of sauvignon blanc in the evening. We cats have no access to everyday mood-enhancing substances. Apart from humble catnip, there is no pharmaceutical refuge if we're suffering from boredom, depression, existential crisis, or even an everyday headache." - David Michie, The Dalai Lama's Cat

"But giving drugs to a cat is no joke, Kemp!" - H G Wells, The Invisible Man

"Catnip is vodka and whiskey to most cats." - Carl Van Vechten

"Wasn't growing catnip in one's yard the kitty equivalent of giving candy to children?" - Caroline Paul, Lost Cat: A True Story of Love, Desperation, and GPS Technology

"I'm an artist; affirmation is like catnip to me." - Andrea Riseborough

"You cannot have more catnip! You have a catnip problem!" - Buffy the Vampire Slayer

"If you don't talk to your cat about catnip, who will?" - Unknown

"Talk to your cat about catnip." - Unknown

"On the edge of a laughing teacup
Did Kubla Kat decree
The corn fritter festooned with medals
Shall make the brownies free
And so the walls turned to water
To let our sorrows drown
As the chairs burned themselves for warmth
So they need not face the clown
Then the spoons burst into song
And all the forks they understood
As I stared at my talking claws
Because this catnip is just that good" - Francesco
Marciuliano, I Could Pee on This And Other Poems
by Cats

"Warning! Catnip may cause purranoia." -
Unknown

"Legalize Catnip." - Unknown

"Dogs are high on life. Cats need catnip." - Eloisa
James

"We got some catnip that'll set you free." - Hall and
Oates, Alley Katz

"Tasty like bean dip, frisky like catnip." - Digital
Underground, Wind Me Up

"Human, I think it is time for your purrformance
evaluation...food and cuddling are great...but I am
concerned about the decreased number of boxes,

lack of sticks with feathers and the overall decline in catnip." - Unknown feline

"Catnip is meowijuana." - Unknown

"I'm gay catnip." - Cher

Particular Breeds

"...if you've never been cussed out by a Siamese, you don't know what profanity is all about!" - Lilian Jackson Braun

"All cats are republicans. They hate change. Except Siamese, of course. Siamese are Hobbesian monarchists." - Emilie Glover

"No man ever dared to manifest his boredom so insolently as does a Siamese tomcat when he yawns in the face of his amorously importunate wife." - Aldous Huxley

"Four little Persians, but only one looked in my direction. I extended a tentative finger and two soft paws clung to it. There was a contented sound of purring, I suspect on both our parts." - George Freedley

"Siamese Cats have a way of staring at you. Those who have walked in on the Queen cleaning her teeth will know the expression." - Douglas Adams

"Breeding purebred cats is like searching for perfection." - Melissa Bateson

"The statuesque Egyptian Mau silhouetted in the evening dusk quickly transports you to the pyramids of ancient Egypt." - Dot Brocksom

"The Black Cat protects home and family from superstition." - Laurent Ruquier

"The really great thing about cats is their endless variety. One can pick a cat that will fit almost any kind of decor, color, scheme, income, personality, mood. But under the fur, whatever color it may be, there still lies, essentially unchanged, one of the world's free souls." - Eric Gurney

"Egyptian Maus are loving and fiercely loyal companions who want to be at your side and involved in every aspect of your life. They often express their happiness by chortling and trilling in a soft melodious voice and with their tails quivering while treading on their forepaws." - Peter Lamb

"People who belong to Siamese cats must make up their minds to do a good deal of waiting upon them." - Sir Compton Mackenzie

"The modern Egyptian domestic cat, which one encounters in the cafes and bazaars, in the noisy streets of Cairo and in the dusty sun-drenched villages, is a graceful delicate little creature, usually much smaller than Western cats." - Jaromir Malek

"I have a lovely white lady called Snow. It is a pretty breed cat, and I embrace her all day on her pink nose. She wipes out my lines with her tail, walking around the table while I write." - Stephane Mallarme

"Thai-Puss is, I fear, an irredeemably selfish cat. Like other great beauties he demands, rather than deserves, to be forgiven." - Val Gielgud

"What, I sometimes ask, will they think of to ruin next? Why do they always pick on something that might one day, if they hadn't mucked it up, have been valuable? Why on earth, with all the experience we've had, do we go on having Siamese cats? Then I see Sass's blue eyes looking up at me out of that anxious, pointed face - and I pick him up and hug him. That is my answer." - Doreen Tovey

"You know I'm the first rapper to adopt a tabby cat. You know I adopted straight from the ASPCA, you feel me? Just breaking the boundaries, man, showing everybody it's okay to be yourself. Embrace yourself. Embrace your health. Ayyy! Just continue to love yourself and accept." - Brandon McCartney

"Sophronia and Dimity took a vacant love seat at the front, Sophronia dislodging a large, fluffy cat with a scrunched-up face. The cat gave her a disgusted look. Or seemed to; it was hard to tell with that face." - Gail Carriger, Waistcoats & Weaponry

"There were fat cats and skinny cats. The long-tailed and the bobbed. The daring young leapers, and the old windowsill sleepers. Balls of waddling fluff, smooth-coated prowlers, and hairless ones that looked fragile and wise. The tiger-striped, the ring-tailed, and the ones with matching coloured socks and mittens. There were tabbies and calicos. Manx and Persians. Siamese and Bombay. Ragdolls and Birmans. Maine Coons and Russian Blues. There were Snowshoes and Somalis, Tonkinese and Turkish, and many, many more. Brown and beige and orange and grey and black and white and silver cats, each with gleaming eyes of emerald, or sapphire, or amber. A rainbow of precious stones." - Brooke Burgess, The Cat's Maw

"When Mother Nature saw fit to remove the tail of the Manx, she left, in place of the tail, more cat." - Mary E Stewart

"Tabby Cat: The only breed cat you can buy in supermarkets because their integrated bar code facilitates the checkout." - Marc Escayrol

"A third of abandoned cats are black cats." - Laurent Ruquier

"It is a small black cat, cheeky as a page.
I let it play on my table, often.
Sometimes he sits down without making a fuss;
Looking like a nice paperweight alive." - Edmond Rostand

"The white cat on the white chair lives white minutes I'm not even in." - Naomi Shihab Nye

"Mice are not superstitious because they know very well that they can also be eaten by a white cat." - Patrick Sebastien

"As far as I am concerned, I will never be the adoring and imploring slave of a Persian cat, but I like to think that Persian cats consider us all as their servants. They do not lack nerve. It is this nerve that enchants me." - Frederic Vitoux

"This cat was a remarkably strong and beautiful animal, entirely black, and of wonderful sagacity. Speaking of his intelligence, my wife, who at heart was not a little imbued with superstition, made frequent allusions to the ancient belief that regarded all black cats as witches in disguise." - Edgar Allan Poe

"I remember a night in a villa on the Florentine hills, a green Florentine night... a dumb curiosity seized two of us and caused us to leave our chairs on the loggia where the faint breeze flickered the flames of the Roman lamps and the tall bottles of golden strega stood half-filled, to mount the stairs, led on a nameless questioning, and to seek the chamber directly above the spot where we had been sitting, the temporary abode of two white Persian cats... The room was empty when we entered; the bright moonlight streaming in from the doorway which led to a terrace which formed the roof of the loggia told us that. Noiselessly, and apparently unreasonably, we stole carefully across the broad chamber and looked out... I can still see the expression of horror on my companion's face, perhaps reflected on my own, as we stood just hidden by the hangings at the doorway and saw the two cats softly lift their paws from two white doves who rose unsteadily, dizzily, and lazily into the green atmosphere, while the cats rolled on their backs, stretching their claws to the air and making faint mews..." - Carl Van Vechten

The fine art of cat washing

"Anybody who doesn't know what soap tastes like never washed a cat." - Franklin P Jones

"To bathe a cat takes brute force, perseverance, courage of conviction - and a cat. The last ingredient is usually the hardest to come by." - Stephen Baker

"A cat determined not to be found can fold itself up like a pocket handkerchief if it wants to." - Louis J Camuti

"I don't think it is so much the actual bath that most cats dislike; I think it's the fact that they have to spend a good part of the day putting their hair back in place." - Debbie Peterson

"Places to look: behind the books in the bookshelf, any cupboard with a gap too small for any cat to squeeze through, the top of anything sheer, under anything too low for a cat to squash under and inside the piano." - Roseanne Ambrose-Brown

"Aubrey, crouching on a nearby counter, watched me with squinty eyes, apparently pondering why anyone would willingly immerse themselves in water ever, let alone for extended periods of time." - Richelle Mead, Succubus Blues

"Cat bathing as a martial art." - Unknown

"The cat Bastet sat perched on the rim of the tub, watching me through slitted golden eyes. She was fascinated by baths. I suppose the total immersion in water must have seemed to her a peculiar method of cleansing oneself." - Elizabeth Peters

"Use the element of surprise." - Unknown

"In a single liquid motion, shut the bathroom door, step into the tub enclosure, slide the glass door shut, dip the cat in the water and squirt him with shampoo. You have now begun one of the wildest 45 seconds of your life." - Unknown

"He will usually have nothing to say for about three weeks and will spend a lot of time sitting with his back to you...but at least now he smells a lot better." - Unknown

"I gave my cat a bath the other day... They love it. He sat there, he enjoyed it, it was fun for me. The fur would stick to my tongue, but other than that..." - Steve Martin

Masters of Relaxation

"If there is one spot of sun spilling onto the floor, a cat will find it and soak it up." - Joan Asper McIntosh

"There has never been a cat
Who couldn't calm me down
By walking slowly
Past my chair." - Rod McKuen

"I like cats... When I meet a cat, I say, 'Poor Pussy!' and stoop down and tickle the side of its head; and the cat sticks up its tail in a rigid, cast-iron manner, arches its back, and wipes its nose up against my trousers; and all is gentleness and peace." - Jerome K Jerome, Three Men in a Boat

"I put down my book, The Meaning of Zen, and see the cat smiling into her fur as she delicately combs it with her rough pink tongue. Cat, I would lend you this book to study but it appears you have already read it. She looks up and gives me her full gaze. Don't be ridiculous, she purrs, I wrote it." - Dilys Laing

"Of all animals, the cat alone attains to contemplative life. He regards the wheel of existence from without, like the Buddha." - Andrew Lang

"A cat who sleeps twenty hours a day is perhaps God's best achievement." - Jules Renard

"Cats are connoisseurs of comfort." - James Herriot

"To sit in a comfortable chair means getting there a split second before a cat - and having to suffer the resentful stares as a consequence. It may infiltrate behind you - and shove. Or sit on the arm - and lean. Or wrap itself around your neck - and throttle. Or touch you lightly with persuasive paw or gentle nose... until, of course, you give in." - Pam Brown

"The vanity of man revolts from the serene indifference of the cat." - Agnes Repplier

"The ideal of calm exists in a sitting cat." - Jules Reynard

"It is good to be a cynic - it is better to be a contented cat - and it is best not to exist at all." - H P Lovecraft

"Holding this soft, small living creature in my lap this way, though, and seeing how it slept with complete trust in me, I felt a warm rush in my chest. I put my hand on the cat's chest and felt his heart beating. The pulse was faint and fast, but his heart, like mine, was ticking off the time allotted to his small body with all the restless earnestness of my own." - Haruki Murakami, The Wind-Up Bird Chronicle

"The only thing a cat worries about is what's happening right now. As we tell the kittens, you can only wash one paw at a time." - Lloyd Alexander, Time Cat

"The amazing activity of the cat is delicately balanced by his capacity for relaxation. Every household should contain a cat, not only for decorative and domestic values, but because the cat in quiescence is medicinal to irritable, tense, tortured men and women." - William Lyon Phelps

"I situate myself, and seat myself,
And where you recline I shall recline,
For every armchair belonging to you as good as belongs to me.

"I loaf and curl up my tail
I yawn and loaf at my ease after rolling in the catnip patch." - Henry N Beard, Poetry for Cats: The Definitive Anthology of Distinguished Feline Verse

"Having played to her heart's content, Chibi would come inside and rest for a while. When she began to sleep on the sofa - like a talisman curled gently in the shape of a comma and dug up from a prehistoric archaeological site - a deep sense of happiness arrived, as if the house itself had dreamed this scene." - Takashi Hiraide, The Guest Cat

"... there are things that outweigh comfort, unless one is an old woman or a cat." - Ursula K Le Guin, The Left Hand of Darkness

"The cat is Zen in its essence. Everything else is frivolous." - Frederic Vitoux

"Cats are the sentinels of the invisible." - Louis Velle

"All cats love a cushioned couch." - Jacques Adert

"In these days of tension, human beings can learn a great deal about relaxation from watching a cat, who doesn't just lie down when it is time to rest, but pours his body on the floor and rests in every nerve and muscle." - Murray Robinson

"Let some of the tranquility of the cat curl into me." - David Rowbotham, The Creature in the Chair

"Cats can work out mathematically the exact place to sit that will cause the most inconvenience." - Michael Stevens

"By the time my key hits the lock I hear the soft press of paws on the other side of the door." - Gwen Cooper

"She sat there on the hearthrug... her eyes screwed tight with anticipation, her paws pounding up and down like little pistons." - Doreen Tovey

"You can't look at a sleeping cat and be tense." - Jane Pauley

"A dreamer whose philosophy is sleep and let sleep." - Saki

"Drowsing, they take the noble attitude of a great
sphinx, who, in a desert land, sleeps always,

dreaming dreams that have no end." - Charles Baudelaire

"Cats at firesides live luxuriously and are the picture of comfort." - Leigh Hunt

"A cat can maintain a position of curled up somnolence on your knee until you are nearly upright. To the last minute she hopes your conscience will get the better of you and you will settle down again." - Pam Brown

"Everything a cat is and does physically is to me beautiful, lovely, stimulating, soothing, attractive and an enchantment." - Paul Gallico

"Cats have very sad faces. They look at you a long time and think about you. They are peaceful to have around." - Unknown

"Pussy...symbolically gives a twist of a yawn, and a lick to her whiskers. Now she proceeds to clean herself all over, having a just sense of the demands of her elegant person - beginning judiciously with her paws, and fetching amazing tongues at her hind-hips. Anon, she scratches her neck with a foot of rapid delight; leaning her head towards it, and shutting her eyes, half to accommodate the action of her skin, and half to enjoy the luxury. She then rewards her paws with a few more touches; look at the action of her head and neck, how pleasing it is, the ears pointed forward and the neck gently arching to and fro! Finally she gives a sneeze, and another twist of mouth and whiskers, and then, curling her tail towards her front claws, settles herself on her hind quarters, in an attitude of bland meditation." - Leigh Hunt

"There is nothing sweeter than his peace when at rest. For there is nothing brisker than his life when in motion." - Christopher Smart

"Cats sleep anywhere, any table, any chair..." - Eleanor Farjeon

"All of the animals except for man know that the principle business of life is to enjoy it." - Samuel Butler

"A little drowsing cat is an image of perfect beautitude." - Jules Champfleury

"'You are getting very sleepy' is not a command when said to a cat; it is an eternal truth." - Ari Rapkin

"Has anyone ever had a stroke or a heart attack while cosied up with a pet? I doubt it." - Robert Brault

Mysteriousness

"The city of cats and the city of men exist one inside the other, but they are not the same city." - Italo Calvino

"It always gives me a shiver when I see a cat seeing what I can't see." - Eleanor Farjeon

"Always the cat remains a little beyond the limits we try to set for him in our blind folly." - Andre Norton

"Cats are a mysterious kind of folk. There is more passing in their minds than we are aware of." - Sir Walter Scott

"Behind the handsome face and piercing gaze of the cat there is always that tantalizing, inscrutable something, the exotic and secret centre that harks back to an ancient connection with sacred cults and the black arts." - David Taylor

"You cannot live with a paw in each world." - Erin Hunter, Into the Wild

"Cats, no less liquid than their shadows, offer no angles to the wind. They slip, diminished, neat, through loopholes lesser than themselves." - A S J Tessimond

"The cool, lithe, cynical, and unconquered lord of the housetops." - H P Lovecraft, Cats and Dogs

"What sort of philosophers are we, who know absolutely nothing of the origin and destiny of cats?" - Henry David Thoreau, Thoreau Journal 9

"Through all this horror my cat stalked unperturbed. Once I saw him monstrously perched atop a mountain of bones, and wondered at the secrets that might lie behind his yellow eyes." - H P Lovecraft, The Rats in the Walls

"Are cats strange animals or do they so resemble us that we find them curious as we do monkeys?" - John Steinbeck, The Winter of Our Discontent

"Of all the things God created, from sunrises and rainbows, to black holes and humor, cats are the most fascinating to me." - Jarod Kintz, The Days of Yay are Here! Wake Me Up When They're Over.

"Prowling his own quiet backyard or asleep by the fire, he is still only a whisker away from the wilds." - Jean Burden, Celebration of Cats

"Human beings are drawn to cats because they are all we are not - self-contained, elegant in everything they do, relaxed, assured, glad of company, yet still possessing secret lives." - Pam Brown

"(Love is the puzzle that) can't be solved. Catlike, it follows no rules but its own, and only it knows what they are. Also it can change the rules any time it wants, in any way it wants, and there's nothing

anyone can do about it." - Chris Dee, Cat-Tales
Book 5

"Their [cats] effortless passing between the wild
and domestic worlds suggests the kind of grace we
need as a species to move between nature and
culture." - Richard Mabey, Nature Cure

"Evidence indicates that cats were first tamed in
Egypt. The Egyptians stored grain, which attracted
rodents, which attracted cats. (No evidence that
such a thing happened with the Mayans, though a
number of wild cats are native to the area.) I don't
think this is accurate. It is certainly not the whole
story. Cats didn't start as mousers. Weasels and
snakes and dogs are more efficient as rodent-control
agents. I postulate that cats started as psychic
companions, as Familiars, and have never deviated
from this function." - William S Burroughs, The Cat
Inside

"If a fish is the movement of water embodied, given
shape, then a cat is a diagram and pattern of subtle
air." - Doris Lessing, On Cats

"Cats, no less liquid than their shadows,
Offer no angles to the wind.
They slip, diminished, neat, through loopholes
Less than themselves." - A S J Tessimond,
Collected Poems

"He looked up at the stars as the storm closed in and
saw them extinguished, one-by-one, until just two

remained. They glimmered and shone through gaps in the clouds like two great eyes in the darkness, burning on a demon's face that chased him across the sea." - Brooke Burgess, The Cat's Maw

"It was a fitting animal for a priest. Cats guard the secrets of the otherworld and are liaisons with mystic realms. Protectors of esoteric knowledge, cats can open the gates through which a priest can see the future and gain insight." - M J Rose, Seduction

"Child of the shadows, he appears as tame,
Till, from behind the grate, the gold eyes glare
With such a light as could consume the whole
To ashes and a memory of flame." - Babette Deutsch

"Cats are magical... the more you pet them the longer you both live." - Unknown

"Always turn and look when your cat gazes behind you with that intent look in her eyes. Some day there might actually be something there." - Unknown

"Sometimes he sits at your feet looking into your face with an expression so gentle and caressing that the depth of his gaze startles you. Who can believe that there is no soul behind those luminous eyes!" - Theophile Gautier

"Cats conspire to keep us at arm's length." - Frank
Perkins

"A cat's secrets run so deep that even the cat itself is often unaware. Their mysteries are as natural as whiskers." - Wendy Beck, 9th Life

"Cats are the visible angels of the cities! There is always an eye of a cat observing you somewhere!" - Mehmet Murat Ildan

"A house isn't a home without the ineffable contentment of a cat with its tail folded about its feet. A cat gives mystery, charm, suggestion." - L M Montgomery, Emily's Quest

"Nothin' wrong with havin' a cat in the house. They can see what most people can't, like the folks in the Otherworld when they cross back over - the good ones and the bad. And they get rid a mice." - Kami Garcia, Beautiful Darkness

"Sometimes she could swear that she saw, in Joe Grey's eyes, a judgment far too perceptive, a watchfulness too aware and intense for any cat. Charlie didn't understand what it was about those two [cats]. Both had a presence that set them apart from other felines.
Maybe she just knew them better. Maybe all cats had that quality of awareness, when you knew them." - Shirley Rousseau Murphy, Cat in the Dark

"A cat is a puzzle for which there is no solution." -
Hazel Nicholson

"These enigmatic animals have in their eyes the depth and stars of a piece of sky." - Armand Sylvestre

"It is in their eyes that their magic resides." - Arthur Symons

"When you are a cat, you are the one that goes alone and for which all paths are identical." - Jacques Roubaud

"The cat has a prophetic spirit and ancient Egyptians were right in honouring it." - Pierre de Ronsard

"His company brings the lonely man the comforting balm of mysticism." - Maurice Rollinat

"You see the beauty of the world
Through eyes of unalloyed content,
And in my study chair upcurled,
Move me to pensive wonderment.

I wish I knew the trick of your thought,
The perfect balance of your ways;
They seem an inspiration, caught
From other laws in older days." - Anonymous

"Is it yet another survival of jungle instinct, this hiding away from prying eyes at important times? Or merely a gesture of independence, a challenge to man and his stupid ways?" - Michael Joseph

"It always gives me a shiver when I see a cat seeing what I can't see." - Eleanor Farjeon

"He lives in the halflights in secret places, free and alone - this mysterious little great being whom his mistress calls 'my cat'." - Margaret Benson

"But the quiet life, fundamentally, is not too interesting for a cat. The idea of a cat satisfied with a saucer of milk and a place by the fire is only half the picture. The more important half we can only guess at. It starts where we leave off - in the larger community outdoors." - Lloyd Alexander

"Cats are the visible angels of the cities! There is always an eye of a cat observing you somewhere!" - Mehmet Murat Ildan

"Their eyes are fathomless depths of cat-world mysteries." - Lesley Anne Ivory

"For the cat is cryptic, and close to strange things which men cannot see..." - H P Lovecraft

"All cats can see futures, and see echoes of the past." - Neil Gaiman

"Minnaloushe creeps through the grass
Alone, important and wise
And lifts to the changing moon
His changing eyes." - William Butler Yeats

Wild Cats

"You put quite a fight for a tame kitty." - Erin Hunter, Into the Wild

"A cat is a tiger that is fed by hand." - Yakaoka Genrin

"Cat: A pygmy lion who loves mice, hates dogs, and patronizes human beings." - Oliver Herford

"Prowling his own quiet backyard or asleep by the fire, he is still only a whisker away from the wilds." - Jean Burden

"The phrase 'domestic cat' is an oxymoron." - George F Will

"I think all cats are wild. They only act tame if there's a saucer of milk in it for them." - Douglas Adams

"We tie bright ribbons around their necks, and occasionally little tinkling bells, and we affect to think that they are as sweet and vapid as the coy name 'kitty' by which we call them would imply. It is a curious illusion. For, purring beside our fireplaces and pattering along our back fences, we have got a wild beast as uncowed and uncorrupted as any under heaven." - Alan Devoe

"When they are among us, cats are angels." -
George Sand

"The cat is a wild animal that inhabits the homes of humans." - Konrad Lorenz

"He lives in the half-lights in secret places, free and alone - this mysterious little great being." - Margaret Benson

"Cats, while animals of prey, are useful as domestics; that while showing wisdom, they have more attachments to places than to people; they have light, adroit, clean and voluptuous bodies; they love ease and search out the softest furniture; they take naps all day long and so repose and rest themselves; they are pretty as young cats and possess a very proper way to amuse children (if the strokes of their paws was not to be feared); they seem to have a natural dread of water, cold and bad smells; they are attracted to perfumes and allow themselves to be caressed by people who wear them; and they have eyes that 'imbibe light' by day and give off light at night." - George-Louis Leclerc

"The cat does not negotiate with the mouse." - Robert K Massie

"The clever cat eats cheese and breathes down rat holes with baited breath." - W C Fields

"A cat brings you gifts: half a lizard, an eviscerated squirrel, but she means well." - Leonore Fleischer

"Cats too, with what silent stealthiness, with what light steps do they creep towards a bird!" - Pliny the Elder

"When she walked abroad she stretched out long and thin like a little tiger, and held her head high to look over the grass as if she were treading the jungle." - Sarah Orne Jewett

"A cat's idea of a 'good time' is to kill something." - Andy Rooney

"The cat in gloves catches no mice." - Benjamin Franklin

"Cats of good breed hunt better fat than lean." - Benvenuto Cellini

"All cats were at first wild, but were at length tamed by the industry of Mankind; it is a Beast of prey, even the tame one, more especially the wild, it being in the opinion of many nothing but a diminutive lion." - William Salmon

"A tomcat has it so easy, he has only to spray and his presence is there for years on rainy days." - Albert Einstein

Purrs, Hisses and Meows

"The purr from cat to man says, 'You bring me happiness; I am at peace with you'." - Barbara L Diamond

"From sucking cat to suffering cat, the same note remains. Purring, the cat gives herself body and soul." - Jean-Louis Hue

"A cat can purr its way out of anything." - Donna McCrohan

"To err is human, to purr is feline." - Robert Byrne

"I have noticed that what cats most appreciate in a human being is not the ability to produce food - which they take for granted - but his or her entertainment value. Asmodeus took to his toy enthusiastically. In another week he permitted me to stroke him, producing a raucous purr, but, in order to save his face, pretending to be asleep." - Geoffrey Household, Rogue Male

"Cats were often familiars to workers of magic because to anyone used to wrestling with self-willed, wayward, devious magic - which was what all magic was - it was rather soothing to have all the same qualities wrapped up in a small, furry, generally attractive bundle that... might, if it were in a good mood, sit on your knee and purr. Magic never sat on anybody's knee and purred." - Robin McKinley, Spindle's End

"When the tea is brought at five o'clock
And all the neat curtains are drawn with care,
The little black cat with bright green eyes
Is suddenly purring there." - Harold Monro,
Collected Poems

"Cats make one of the most satisfying sounds in the
world: they purr. Almost all cats make us feel good
about ourselves because they let us know they feel
good about us, about themselves, and about our
relationship with them. A purring cat is a form of
high praise, like a gold star on a test paper. It is a
reinforcement of something we would all like to
believe about ourselves - that we are nice." - Roger
A Caras, A Celebration of Cats

"Sometimes I like her calm, unwild,
gentle as a sleeping child,
and wonder as she lies, a fur ring,
curled upon my lap, unstirring -
is it me or Tibbles purring?" - Ian Serraillier

"Indeed, there is nothing on this earth more peaceful
than a sleeping, purring cat." - Jonathon Scott
Payne, Mighty Little Man: My Story, His Story,
Our Story

"I was just thinking how the purr of a contented cat
is one of my favorite sounds in the world. There's
something so comforting about it, isn't there?" -
Laura Lam, Shadowplay

"Love, you just know it when you feel it. I feel it now, and it's furry and purring." - Jarod Kintz, Love Quotes for the Ages. Specifically Ages 19-91

"No one has ever been able to discover how they make this subtle sound, and what is more, no one ever will. It is a secret that has endured from the very beginning of the time of cats and will never be revealed." - Paul Gallico

"I simply can't resist a cat, particularly a purring one. They are the cleanest, cunningest, and most intelligent things I know, outside of the girl you love, of course."
- Abroad with Mark Twain and Eugene Field, Fisher

"Even if you have just destroyed a Ming Vase, purr. Usually all will be forgiven." - Lenny Rubenstein

"I pet her and she pays me back in purrs." - Terri Guillemets

"Are we really sure the purring is coming from the kitty and not from our very own hearts?" - Terri Guillemets

"If we treated everyone we meet with the same affection we bestow upon our favorite cat, they, too, would purr." - Martin Buxbaum

"If there were to be a universal sound depicting peace, I would surely vote for the purr." - Barbara L Diamond

"No one shall deny me my own conclusions, nor my cat her reflective purr." - Irving Townsend

"Could the purr be anything but contemplative?" - Irving Townsend

"No one shall deny me my own conclusions, nor my cat her reflective purr." - Irving Townsend

"As surely as the cat begins to purr when you stroke his back, as surely we see a sweet ecstasy painted on the figure of the man you praise, especially when the praise is about the scope of his claims, even though it might be a palpable lie." - Arthur Schopenhauer

"Cats speak a subtle language in which few sounds carry many meanings, depending on how they are sung or purred. 'Mnrhnh' means comfortable soft chairs. It also means fish. It means genial companionship... and the absence of dogs." - Val Schaffner

"A cat has to be in a very bad mood if a human cannot coax him to purr." - Derek Tangye, A Cat in the Window

"When I'm discouraged, he's empathy incarnate, purring and rubbing to telegraph his dismay..." - Catheryn Jakobson

"A cat can be trusted to purr when she is pleased, which is more than can be said for human beings." - William Ralph Inge

"Cats are successful underachievers. They only need to purr in order to get free food and TLC. What other creature can lay around the house doing nothing beyond purring, and still get free food and TLC?" - Jim Aites

"The purr from cat to man says, 'You bring me happiness; I am at peace with you.'" - Barbara L Diamond

"No cat purrs unless someone is around to listen." - Elizabeth Marshall Thomas

"With one of the most bewitching sounds in the world, its purr, the cat persuades us that it thinks we're wonderful." Akif Pirincci and Rolf Degen

"Cats are bundles of cute, wrapped in fur and purrs." - Jarod Kintz, This Book Has No Title

"My cat speaks sign language with her tail." - Robert A M Stern

"An animal's eyes have the power to speak a great language." - Martin Buber

"A meow massages the heart." - Stuart McMillan

"If purring could be encapsulated, it'd be the most powerful anti-depressant on the pharmaceutical market." - Terri Guillemets

"Meow is like aloha - it can mean anything." - Hank Ketchum

"Ignorant people think it is the noise which fighting cats make that is so aggravating, but it ain't so; it is the sickening grammar that they use." - Mark Twain

"There is no cat 'language'. Painful as it is for us to admit, they don't need one." - Barbara Holland

"I'm trying to translate what my cat says and put it in a book, but how many homonyms are there for meow?" - Jarod Kintz, The Days of Yay are Here! Wake Me Up When They're Over.

"When I meow it means... I am hungry... I want food in my bowl... I want food in my bowl right now... I want to go out... I want to come in... Brush me... Get my toy out from under the sofa... It's time to change the litter... I just put a mouse in the bureau drawer... I did not break that vase... Get me down from this tree... Please kill that dog next door... Hello... Goodbye." - Henry Beard

"If cats could talk, they wouldn't." - Nan Porter

"Most cats are not shy about letting their people know what they want." - Karen Duprey

"Meow when you feel like it." - Lauren Merryfield's cats

"What part of meow don't you understand?" - Richard Smith

"You had me at meow." - Unknown

Purrsonalities

"A cat's hearing apparatus is such that it allows the human voice to easily go in at one ear and out at the other." - Stephen Baker

"Sky is in her eyes, hell is in her heart." - Honore de Balzac

"Some cats are blind and stone deaf but ain't no cat wuz ever dumb." - Anthony Henderson Euwer

"Good curiosity probably saved many cats." - Carl Barks

"When you are looking at it, a cat acts like a princess, but the very minute it thinks you are not looking, a cat acts like a fool." - KC Buffington

"There is something of the camel about cats." - Rene Chartrand

"Every cat is special in its own way." - Sara Jane Clark

"The great charm of cats is their rampant egotism, their devil- may- care attitude toward responsibility, and their disinclination to earn an honest dollar." - Robertson Davies

"You never saw such a crazy cat. 'Up the wall' took on a literal meaning with him." - Arnold Hano

"Cats are smart. You know it and I know it." - Debbie Mertens

"We cannot, unless we become cats, perfectly understand the cat's mind." - St George Mivart

"We need cats to need us. It unnerves us that they do not. However, if they do not need us, they nonetheless seem to love us." - Jeffrey Moussaieff Masson

"Cats randomly refuse to follow orders to prove they can." - Ilona Andrews, Magic Strikes

"I have a bedroom rug that I feed. It's not very flat, and it meows when I step on it." - Jarod Kintz, This is the best book I've ever written, and it still sucks

"Loud ringing noises, I've discovered, upset Mr Peepers." - Meg Cabot, The Boy Next Door

"If my cat jumps on my knee and I push her off, however, gently... she walks off in high dudgeon. Even immediate repentance is useless... for days she will show her displeasure by ignoring me completely." - Michael Joseph

"When my cats aren't happy, I'm not happy: Not because I care about their mood but because I know they're just sitting there thinking up ways to get even." - Penny Ward Moser

"Cats like doors to be left open - in case they change their minds." - Rosemary Nisbet

"The refusal of cats to understand is deliberate." - Louis Nucera

"Anyone who claims that a cat cannot give a dirty look either has never kept a cat or is singularly unobservant." - Maurice Burton

"Some people say that cats are sneaky, evil and cruel. True - and they have many other fine qualities as well." - Missy Dizick

"The trouble with cats is that they've got no tact." - PG Wodehouse

"A man waits on a cat hand and foot for weeks, humouring its lightest whim, and it goes and leaves him flat because it has found a place down the road where fish is more frequent." - PG Wodehouse

"Cats allow us to love them, for which we should be duly grateful." - Anne Taylor-Browne

"After scolding one's cat one looks into its face and is seized by the ugly suspicion that it understood every word. And has filed it for reference." - Charlotte Gray

"Cats only occupy space and think about three things: food, sex and nothing. If they're neutered that leaves food." - Penny Ward Moser

"You can feel an awful fool standing at the bottom of the garden yelling pussy, pussy, pussy across a totally deserted meadow. Especially when you realize that pussy, pussy, pussy is watching you, with benign interest, from the shelter of the garden shed." - Marcia Fischer

"Out-thinking a cat that doesn't much want to come in, is a refinement of chess." - Dominic Courcel

"A cat likes to hear you calling him. He sits in a bush a yard from your shoes - and listens." - Pam Brown

"If cats could talk, they would lie to you." - Bob Kopack

"Most cats, when they are Out want to be In and vice versa, and often simultaneously." - Dr Louis J Camuti

"It's wonderful how far a cat can elongate its arm when it needs to steal a roasted chicken leg." - Pam Brown

"You only realize too late why the cat was on top of the fridge when you notice how smooth the butter is." - Peter Delaney

"Cats, as a class, have never completely got over the snootiness caused by the fact that in Ancient Egypt they were worshipped as Gods." - P G Wodehouse

"Never try to outstubborn a cat." - Robert A
Heinlein

"There are people who reshape the world by force or argument, but the cat just lies there, dozing, and the world quietly reshapes itself to suit his comfort and convenience." - Allen and Ivy Dodd

"If its raining at the back door every cat is convinced there's a good chance it won't be raining at the front door." - William Toms

"There is nothing so lowering to one's self-esteem as the affectionate contempt of a beloved cat." - Agnes Repplier

"Cats are absolute individuals, with their own ideas about everything, including the people they own." - John Dingman

"The fact is that, to cats, we humans are, for all our grotesque size, unbelievably slow and clumsy. We are totally incapable of managing a good leap or jump or pounce or swipe or indeed, any other simple maneuver which, at the very least, would make us passable fun to play with." - Cleveland Amory

"Cats do not go for a walk to get somewhere but to explore." - Sidney Denham

"Of all God's creatures, there is only one that cannot be made slave of the leash. That one is the cat. If man could be crossed with the cat it would improve the man, but it would deteriorate the cat." - Mark Twain

"The way to get on with a cat is to treat it as an equal - or even better, as the superior it knows itself to be." - Elizabeth Peters, The Snake, the Crocodile and the Dog

"I am what I am. I would tell you what you want to know if I could, for you have been kind to me. But I am a cat, and no cat anywhere ever gave anyone a straight answer." - Peter S Beagle, The Last Unicorn

"'Such nonsense!' declared Dr Greysteel. 'Whoever heard of cats doing anything useful!'
'Except for staring at one in a supercilious manner,' said Strange. 'That has a sort of moral usefulness, I suppose, in making one feel uncomfortable and encouraging sober reflection upon one's imperfections.'" - Susanna Clarke, Jonathan Strange & Mr Norrell

"A cat's rage is beautiful, burning with pure cat flame, all its hair standing up and crackling blue sparks, eyes blazing and sputtering." - William S Burroughs, The Cat Inside

"When Rome burned, the emperor's cats still expected to be fed on time." - Seanan McGuire, Rosemary and Rue

"A cat is more intelligent than people believe, and
can be taught any crime." - Mark Twain

"I like how cats' ears can flip inside out. It's as if they're saying, Keep talking, human, but I'm not even listening." - Jarod Kintz, This is the best book I've ever written, and it still sucks

"When a cat flatters... he is not insincere: you may safely take it for real kindness." - Walter Savage Landor, Imaginary Conversations

"Cats have a sort of game they play when they meet. A player alternates between watching the strange cat and ignoring her, grooming or examining everything around herself - a dead leaf, a cloud - with complete absorption. It is almost accidental how the two cats approach, a sidelong step and then the sitting again. This often ends in a flurry of spitting and slashing claws, too fast to see clearly, and then one or the other (or both) of the cats leap out of range. The game can have one exchange or many - and is not so different from the first meetings of women." - Kij Johnson, Fudoki

"Cats ask plainly for what they want." - Walter Savage Landor, Imaginary Conversations

"Then it suddenly and theatrically began to clean itself in the way cats do when they want you to know what a big deal you aren't." - Adam Rex, Cold Cereal

"He inclined his head ever so slightly, displaying with his bearing the supreme confidence, even arrogance, that is the sole providence of cats, dragons, and certain highborn women." - Christopher Paolini, Inheritance

"Cats don't think they're owned by anybody. Even behind doors and windows, like amiable Wally, they're free. Always.
That may, in fact, be the most important thing about them." - Michael Korda

"Desire, problem solving, and communication are all signs of intelligence and awareness. My cat has these, so it's quite possible he has a soul too." - Lewis N Roe, From A To Theta: Taking The Tricky Subject Of Religion And Explaining Why It Makes Sense In A Way We Can All Understand

"The cat is beauty and the beast, a baffling blend, a wicked feast.
For all who dream of varied light, the cat holds both the dark and bright." - Wendy Beck, 9th Life

"The approval of a cat cannot but flatter the recipient." - Elizabeth Peters, The Snake, the Crocodile and the Dog

"We are the cats inside. We are the cats who cannot walk alone, and for us there is only one place." - William S. Burroughs, The Cat Inside

"My cat is always looking at me like I am forgetting something crucial and he depends on it." - Megan

Boyle, Selected Unpublished Blog Posts of a Mexican Panda Express Employee

"Nothing snubs quite like a cat. What evolutionary purpose did it serve, this inherent disdain, this artful blanking?" - Will Wiles, Care of Wooden Floors

"Alice: I didn't know that Cheshire Cats grinned. In fact, I didn't know that cats could grin.

Duchess: They can, and most of 'em do." - Rod Espinosa, Alice in Wonderland

"Don't judge a cat by its coat." - Magdalena VandenBerg

"Cats can be cooperative when something feels good, which, to a cat, is the way everything is supposed to feel as much of the time as possible." - Roger Caras

"Some people say man is the most dangerous animal on the planet. Obviously those people have never met an angry cat." - Lillian Johnson

"Cats are notoriously sore losers. Coming in second best, especially to someone as poorly coordinated as a human being, grates their sensibility." - Stephen Baker

"A cat's behavior is a direct reflection of his feelings." - Carole Wilbourn

"The constant challenge of deciphering feline behavior is perhaps one of the most fascinating aspects of owning a cat." - Carole Wilbourn

"A cat doesn't accustom himself well to change if it is someone else's making." - Carole Wilbourn

"A cat is never vulgar." - Carl Van Vechten

"Cats are smart and aware of it." - Tomi Ungerer

"The cat, however clean he is, though already well-combed, preens himself with great care." - Maurice Rollinat

"The cat in gloves catches no mice." - Franklin Delano Roosevelt

"One reason we admire cats is their proficiency in one-upmanship. They always seem to come out on top." - Barbara Webster

"One is never sure, watching two cats washing each other, whether it's affection, the taste or a trial run for the jugular." - Helen Thomson

"Cats' hearing apparatus is built to allow the human voice to easily go in one ear and out the other." - Stephen Baker

"Lettin' the cat out of the bag is a whole lot easier'n puttin' it back in." - Will Rogers

"Caresses never turned a tiger into a kitten." -
Franklin Delano Roosevelt

"The cat does not caress us, she caresses herself against us." - Antoine de Rivarol

"Cats have uncommon personalities." - Christopher Paolini

"Mice amused him, but he usually considered them too small game to take seriously; I have seen him play for an hour with a mouse and then let it go with a royal condescension." - Charles Dudley Warner

"A cat's got her own opinion of human beings. She don't say much, but you can tell enough to make you anxious not to hear the whole of it." - Jerome K Jerome

"Cats always seem so very wise, when staring with their half-closed eyes." - Bette Midler

"Oh I am a cat who likes to gallop about doing good." - Stevie Smith

"When you are looking, a cat acts like a princess, but the minute they think you are not looking, a cat acts like a fool." - K C Buffington

"Some animals are secretive; some are shy. A cat is private." - Leonard Michaels

"It is remarkable in cats, that the outer life they reveal to their masters is one of perpetual boredom." - Robley Wilson, Jr

"A cat doesn't 'roll' well with a change of someone else's making." - Carole Wilbourn

"Many cats simply pounce to their own drummers."
- Karen Duprey

"Among animals, cats are the top-hatted, frock-coated statesmen going about their affairs at their own pace." - Robert Sterns

"Cats do not wear their hearts on their sleeves, which is not to say that they do not miss you when you are away. However, they feel that you have behaved very badly and may not be very civil to you when you return. After you have apologized, normal relations can be resumed." - Susanne Millen

"Cats can obviously rise to considerable mental heights, at least when they want to satisfy their lower instincts." - Akif Pirincci and Rolf Degen

"Anyone who has lived on terms of comparative equality with a cat knows he will show his intelligence fifty times a day. To be sure this intelligence is usually of the variety called selfish."
- Carl Van Vechten

"If the cat waits for long hours, silent beside the crack of the wainscot, it is for pure pleasure. Cats do not keep the mice away; it is my belief that they preserve them for the chase." - Oswald Barron

"Another and very different gesture, expressive of pleasure, has already been described, namely, the curious manner in which young and even old cats, when pleased, alternately protrude their fore-feet, with separated toes, as if pushing against and sucking their mother's teats. This habit is so far analogous to that of rubbing against something, that both apparently are derived from actions performed during the nursing period." - Charles Darwin

"You know what cats are like - fast on their feet and not very grateful." - Helen Magee

"Cats are by nature very stubborn and may resist what they learn and already know when it interferes with their essential character as voluptuaries." - Roger Caras

"The two cats never fought, physically. They fought great duels with their eyes." - Doris Lessing

"Cats virtually always underestimate human intelligence just as we, perhaps, underestimate theirs." - Roger Caras

"Q: Where does a two-thousand-pound gorilla sleep? A: Anywhere it wants to. Q: Where does a ten-pound cat sleep? A: Anywhere it wants to." - Leonore Fleischer

"In my house lives a cat who is a curmudgeon and cantankerous, a cat who is charming and convivial, and a cat who is combative and commendable. And yet I have but one cat." David Edwards

"One reason that cats are happier than people is that they have no newspapers." - Gwendolyn Brooks, In the Mecca

Strays

"Most cats do not approach humans recklessly. The possibility of concealed weapons, clods or sticks, tend to make them reserved. Homeless cats in particular - with some justification, unfortunately - consider humans their natural enemies. Much ceremony must be observed, and a number of diplomatic feelers put out, before establishing a state of truce." - Lloyd Alexander

"If a homeless cat could talk, it would probably say, 'Give me shelter, food, companionship and love, and I will be yours for life!'" - Susan Easterly

"Whenever a mistress leaves me, I adopt an alley cat: an animal leaves, another comes." - Paul Leautaud

"Household garbage attracts rats and mice. These three elements constitute a reserve of food for feral cats and can form the center of activity of a group." - Suzan Lumpkin

"Kittens always manage to find a home. They stray about outside your house looking cute and vulnerable until they break down your defences. Then they take over - completely." - Lisa Scully O'Grady

"If a stray kitten bounds out of nowhere when you're taking a walk, mews piteously, and rubs a soft shoulder against your leg, flee to the hills until the danger is over." - Murray Robinson

"Round, misty-blue eyes stare desperately from the cardboard box. Love me, they say, feed me, warm me, care for me, let me into your life - so that I can begin to take over your existence." - Pam Brown

"The cat of the slums and alleys, starved, outcast, harried, still displays the self-reliant watchfulness which man has never taught it to lay aside." - Saki

"Suddenly a pair of eyes appeared, glowing in the dark. A moment later a huge cat jumped on to the counter. His body was thin but muscular, and his claws seemed enormous. A shaggy mane haloed his angular face. His ears were dotted with black tufts. Under his coat, one guessed a powerful jaw." - Christopher Paolini

"I cannot honestly report that I have ever seen a feline matron of this class (alley) washing her face when in an interesting condition." - Charles Dickens

"I want to create a cat like the real cats I see crossing the streets, not like those you see in houses. They have nothing in common. The cat of the streets has bristling fur. It runs like a fiend, and if it looks at you, you think it is going to jump in your face." - Pablo Picasso

"He collected the stray cats. He did not take account
of their faults. He sought distraction." - James
Ellroy

"Often at shelters, we hear, 'I told my child she could get a pet, but she will have to take care of him.' That is an unrealistic expectation and often results in the pet being returned days, weeks, or months later. It is hard for pets to go in and out of a home. They bond with their humans and when they find themselves at a shelter, they become stressed at being taken away from home and the people they love. When an 'easy-way-out' decision is made to give up a pet, we are teaching our children that animals can be given away, turned away, and gotten rid of at the drop of a hat. If you are considering getting a cat or kitten, go into it fully aware that the adults in the home will have to help with the care of the pet." - Carol Griglione, Animal Rescue League of Iowa for Love of Cats: A Hands on Journey

"'You know, Professor, this stray kitten and you have one very important thing in common.'
'I can't imagine,' responded the professor coolly.
'Your life is the most important thing in the world to you,' said His Holiness. 'Same for this kitten'." - David Michie, The Dalai Lama's Cat

"There are tramp dogs but no tramp cats. When a cat sees that his master can no longer afford to feed him, he abandons him to find another more fortunate. While dogs are what they are but they remain faithful to their master, even if poor, until death." - Bernard Werber

"Much ceremony must be observed, and a number of diplomatic feelers put out, before establishing a state of truce." - Lloyd Alexander

"The beast was brought in the evening. It didn't make a good impression then, but in the morning, in the full light of day, it looked even worse. It was exorbitantly ugly, that cat. Skinny as a nail, with a long head like a pike and, to add to the picture, black lips; it was an in-elegant ash-gray colour, and its coat was dull and dry. Its bald tail resembled a string with a tuft on the end, and the fur on its belly, which had doubtlessly been skinned in some accident, dangled like bits of fluff swept up from a carpet. Despite its large caressing eyes, in whose emerald depths swirled flecks of gold, its poverty-stricken and dubious coat marked it as a low son of the gutter, an unacceptable cat. But this unacceptable cat, I accepted, because he showed himself willing to be caressed. I looked after him, and I baptized him with the name 'Mouche'." - Joris-Karl Huysmans

"Cats I scorn, who sleek and fat,
Shiver at a Norway Rat;
Rough and Hardy, bold and free,
Be the cat that's made for me!" - Erasmus Darwin

"When he moved, he didn't limp like any ordinary, normal cat, he went round in anguished, three-legged leaps like a frog." - Doreen Tovey

Beautiful Beasts

"Seen from a distance, cats are beautiful. Close up they are a thing of incomparable splendor. In all their actions is perfection." - Pam Brown

"A drowsing little cat is an image of perfect beatitude." - Jules Champfleury

"Two things are aesthetically perfect in the world - the clock and the cat." - Emile-Auguste Chartier

"Deep down, the cat is cat. That's what makes him so beautiful." - Didier Hallepee

"A cat is a living work of art." - Patricia Highsmith

"Cats are living adornments." - Edwin Lent

"There are beauties that are beyond words. Cats belong to this order." - Louis Nucera

"Cats never strike a pose that isn't photogenic." - Lillian Jackson Braun

"Even overweight cats instinctively know the cardinal rule: when fat, arrange yourself in slim poses." - John Weitz

"A cat is only technically an animal, being divine." - Robert Lynd

"Her function is to sit and be admired." - Georgina
Strickland Gates

"When she walked... she stretched out long and thin like a little tiger, and held her head high to look over the grass as if she were treading the jungle." - Sarah Orne Jewett

"God made the cat to give man the pleasure of stroking a tiger." - Francois Joseph Mery

"The only purpose of cats is that they constitute mobile decorative objects, a concept which I find intellectually interesting, but unfortunately our cats have such drooping bellies that this does not apply to them." - Muriel Barbery, The Elegance of the Hedgehog

"The cat is such a perfect symbol of beauty and superiority that it seems scarcely possible for any true aesthete and civilized cynic to do other than worship it." - H P Lovecraft, Cats and Dogs

"The cat... is for the man who appreciates beauty as the one living force in a blind and purposeless universe." - H P Lovecraft, Cats and Dogs

"A garden without cats, it will be generally agreed, can scarcely deserve to be called a garden at all...much of the magic of the heather beds would vanish if, as we bent over them, there was no chance that we might hear a faint rustle among the blossoms, and find ourselves staring into a pair of sleepy green eyes." - Beverley Nichols, Garden Open Tomorrow

"Then the cow asked:
'What is a mirror?'
'It is a hole in the wall,' said the cat. 'You look in it,
and there you see the picture, and it is so dainty and
charming and ethereal and inspiring in its
unimaginable beauty that your head turns round and
round, and you almost swoon with ecstasy.'" - Mark
Twain, Short Stories

"Cats sleep fat and walk thin." - Rosalie Moore

"Of all the domestic animals the cat is the most
expressive. His face is capable of showing a wide
range of expressions. His tail is a mirror of his
mind. His gracefulness is surpassed only by his
agility. And, along with all of these, he has a sense
of humour." - Walter Chandoha

"If God created man in his own image, you've got to
wonder in whose image did he create the cat, a
more noble creature?" - Unknown

"It is with the approach of winter that cats... wear
their richest coats and assume an air of sumptuous
and delightful opulence." - Pierre Loti

"The cat is the animal to whom the Creator gave the
biggest eye, the softest fur, the most supremely
delicate nostrils." - Colette

"I thought she was the loveliest animal I had ever
seen." - Doreen Tovey

"Like a graceful vase, a cat, even when motionless, seems to flow." - George F Will

"There's no need for a piece of sculpture in a home that has a cat." - Wesley Bates

"It was a simple white and gray ball, light as a foam ball, with perfectly round blue eyes." - Fred Vargas

"Subtle combination of grace, elegance and power, this cat with his legendary past will fill you with his tenderness, his softness and his unlimited faithfulness.
You will be stunned by the surprising contrast between his coat naturally spotted, short and glossy and his bright green eyes." - Marylene Roulier

"It seduces us with his grace and beauty, and his movements are elegant, smooth and precise. His glaze fascinates, and so does this hieratic immobility that can turn in a few tenths of a second into power and violence, making the sleeper into a formidable hunter." - Pierre Rousselet-Blanc

"Her skin was the color of blond honey, her face that of a cat, and she moved with grace, flexibility and power that reflected her ease in battle and her natural strength." - Christopher Paolini

"There are beauties that are beyond words. Cats belong to this order." - Louis Nucera

"A cat improves the garden wall in sunshine, and the hearth in foul weather." - Judith Merkle Riley

"I saw the most beautiful cat today. It was sitting by the side of the road, its two front feet neatly and graciously together. Then it gravely swished around its tail to completely encircle itself. It was so fit and beautifully neat, that gesture, and so self-satisfied, so complacent." - Anne Morrow Lindbergh

"Cats are always elegant." - John Weitz

"To respect the cat is the beginning of the aesthetic sense." - Erasmus Darwin

"Cats are the ultimate narcissists. You can tell this because of all the time they spend on personal grooming." - James Gorman

"Its tail was a plume of such magnificence that it almost wore the cat." - Hugh Leonard

"The eyes of a cat will wax and wane with the phases of the moon." - W B Yeats

"A cat's rage is beautiful, burning with pure cat flame, all its hair standing up and crackling blue sparks, eyes blazing and sputtering." - William S Burroughs

"Cats are a tonic, they are a laugh, they are a cuddle, they are at least pretty just about all of the time and beautiful some of the time." - Roger Caras

"It's an honor to paint cats." - Oliver Johnson

The cat has been described as the most perfect animal, the acme of muscular perfection and the supreme example in the animal kingdom of the coordination of mind and muscle." - Roseanne Ambrose-Brown

"Cats only assume their strangest, most intriguing and most beautiful postures when it is impossible to photograph them. Cat calendars always disappoint for they only show the public range of cat positions." - J R Coulson

"There was something theatrical and grandiloquent about him, and he seemed to pose like an actor who attracts admiration. His motions were slow, undulating, and full of majesty; he seemed always to be stepping on a table covered with china ornaments and Venetian glass, so circumspectly did he select the place where he put down his foot." - Theophile Gautier

"Obese cats are far less common than obese dogs (or obese people)." - Desmond Morris

"Class she certainly was, from her tapered black head, beautiful as an Egyptian queen carved out of ebony, to the tip of her elegant whip tail." - Doreen Tovey

"How could I help but be smitten with his scraggly little blackness..." - Patricia Khuly

"A thing of beauty, strength and grace lies behind that whiskered face." - Unknown

It's a Cat's Life

"Cats have it all - admiration, an endless sleep, and company only when they want it." - Rod McKuen

"Guilt isn't in cat vocabulary. They never suffer remorse for eating too much, sleeping too long or hogging the warmest cushion in the house. They welcome every pleasurable moment as it unravels and savour it to the full until a butterfly or falling leaf diverts their attention. They don't waste energy counting the number of calories they've consumed or the hours they've frittered away sunbathing.

"Cats don't beat themselves up about not working hard enough. They don't get up and go, they sit down and stay. For them, lethargy is an art form. From their vantage points on top of fences and window ledges, they see the treadmills of human obligations for what they are - a meaningless waste of nap time." - Helen Brown, Cleo

"Cats are like walking brooms you can actually comfortably cuddle with." - Jarod Kintz, 99 Cents For Some Nonsense

"This is a cat's world, and man's just allowed to share in it." - Jarod Kintz, Seriously delirious, but not at all serious

"Cats may walk by themselves, but there are times when they need our support." - Dr Nicholas Dodman

"Nature abhors a vacuum, but not as much as a cat
does." - Unknown

"I mean to say, we all sprang from humble origins. Goodness gracious, who would have thought that a species of monkey would take over the kingdom of the world. ... I cannot help but feel that the monkey was not a good choice. Surely one of the cat family would have been much more satisfactory. They have a much less emotional approach to life." - Ronald Chetwynd-Hayes

"Yawn. String-on-a-stick.
Fine. I'll come out and chase it
to make you happy." - Lee Wardlaw, Won-Ton: A Cat Tale Told in Haiku

"'Are there any capitalist cats?' Nakata asked." - Haruki Murakami, Kafka on the Shore

"Sunday, January 27, 1884. - There was another story in the paper a week or so since. A gentleman had a favourite cat whom he taught to sit at the dinner table where it behaved very well. He was in the habit of putting any scraps he left onto the cat's plate. One day puss did not take his place punctually, but presently appeared with two mice, one of which it placed on its master's plate, the other on its own." - Beatrix Potter, Beatrix Potter's Journal

"Why so scrawny, cat?
Starving for fat fish or mice...
Or backyard love?" - Matsuo Basho, Japanese Haiku

"Cat: a pygmy lion who loves mice, hates dogs, and patronizes human beings." - Oliver Herford

"The white cat Sal-al was lying on the straw matting in the empty conservatory. She looked at us with a wicked, conceited expression as if all her appetites had just been satisfied. She was beautiful. Vesta and I both said, 'I wish I were a cat!' Before we got to the last word we smiled at each other in annoyance, not liking the idea that most human beings think very much alike." - Denton Welch, Maiden Voyage

"'Not fooling around, not bothering nobody, just sitting here mending the Primus,' said the cat with a hostile frown, 'and, moreover, I consider it my duty to warn you that the cat is an ancient, inviolable animal.'" - Mikhail Bulgakov, The Master and Margarita

"A cat knows how to be comfortable, how to get the people around it to serve it. In a tranquil domestic situation, the cat is a veritable manipulative genius. It seeks the soft, it seeks the warm, it prefers the quiet and it loves to be full. It displays, when it gets its own way in these matters, a degree of contentment we would all like to emulate." - Roger A Caras, A Celebration Of Cats

"In Egypt: Under no conditions, under threat of death could anyone kill a cat. People were exceuted for even killing a cat accidentally. And when a cat died, the whole family, and probably their closest friends, went into mourning, the measure of their personal loss signalled by their shaving off their eyebrows." - Roger A Caras, A Celebration Of Cats

"One upside of the heat. Kind of cool to see a cat pant." - Jonah Goldberg

"[Cats] are blissfully unaware that they have only a finite time in which to finish their 'to do' list." - Jon Edgell, Resolution

"Most people, when they move, well they just move depending on whatever's around them. At this very moment, as I am writing, Constitution the cat is going by with her tummy dragging close to the floor. This cat has absolutely nothing constructive to do in life and still she is heading toward something, probably an armchair."
- Muriel Barbery, The Elegance of the Hedgehog

"The final war will be between Pavlov's dog and Schrödinger's Cat." - Robert Anton Wilson

"If the pull of the outside world is strong, there is also a pull towards the human. The cat may disappear on its own errands, but sooner or later, it returns once again for a little while, to greet us with its own type of love." - Lloyd Alexander

"Life is like cat vomit; if you do not clean it right away, you'll walk in it." - Xnterna

"Love knows all paths, where even gods and cats are blind." - F T McKinstry, Water Dark

"The world would probably be better if people were put in carriers and cats roamed free." - Mary Matthews, Splendid Summer

"I had a dream about you. I was a cat. You were a red dot. And even those times I caught you, we couldn't touch. But still I chased you anyway." - Ryan Lilly, We Had A #Dream About You

"If cats could count, they'd start getting nervous around the time they put paid to their fifth life." - John Connolly, The Wolf in Winter

"Cats will be cats." - Morrissey, Autobiography

"One can imagine that if humanity suddenly disappeared from the planet, the cat would shrug its shoulders, raise its tail, and return to its forest habitat, there to live as its ancestors have done for two million years, forever in search of something small, furry, and squeaky to play with." - Eric Chaline

"Being a cat means beautiful, agile, innocent, brave, curious and trust also honorable respect for as much as not so doing bribery." - Sekar Arum

"The cat arrived with a bottle of Scotch." - Christopher S. Wren, The Cat Who Covered the World: The Adventures Of Henrietta And Her Foreign Correspondent

"She hops expectantly into the sink. I turn on the tap for her; she laps without a glance in my direction, like a duchess so used to being ministered to that she no longer notices the servants and sees only a world where objects dumbly bend to her wishes, doors opening, faucets discharging cool water, delicious things appearing in her dish." - Peter Trachtenberg, Another Insane Devotion: On The Love of Cats and Persons

"The nature of the universe probably depends heavily on who is the actual protagonist. Lately I've been suspecting it's one of my cats." - Wil McCarthy

"For he will do
As he do do
And there's no doing anything about it!" - T S Eliot, Old Possum's Book of Practical Cats

"Even gods decay. Like, in 1890 somebody sold off thousands of mummified Ancient Egyptian sacred cats - _for fertilizer_. Get the point? Constancy isn't." - Jonathan Gash, Jade Woman

"With the qualities of cleanliness, affection, patience, dignity, and courage that cats have, how many of us, I ask you, would be capable of becoming cats?" - Fernand Mery

"She feels happy as a cat treading on velvet paws over the heads of humans." - Bernard Werber

"I think one reason we admire cats, those of us who do, is their proficiency in one-upmanship. They always seem to come out on top, no matter what they are doing-or pretend to do. Rarely do you see a cat discomfited. They have no conscience, and they never regret anything. Maybe we secretly envy them." - Barbara Webster

"The cat seldom interferes with other people's rights. His intelligence keeps him from doing many of the foolish things that complicate life." - Carl Van Vechten

"Fear is a slinking cat I find beneath the lilacs of my mind." - Sophie Tunnel

"A cat sees no good reason why it should obey another animal, even if it does stand on two legs." - Sarah Thomson

"It is in the nature of cats to do a certain amount of unescorted roaming." - Adlai Stevenson

"All is well that ends well in the world of cats." - Jacques Sternberg

"In my next life I want to come back as one of my cats. They basically pretend we don't exist. They sit like two bumps on a log and watch us work for hours in the yard. They're probably wondering, along with the entire neighborhood, why we work so hard in our garden and it still looks like hell." - Annie Spiegelman

"Cats don't adopt people. They adopt refrigerators." - Solomon Short

"Everything I know I learned from my cat: When you're hungry, eat. When you're tired, nap in a sunbeam. When you go to the vet's, pee on your owner." - Gary Smith

"Often we see cats back from the harbour with a fish in their mouths, sometimes still alive." - Hans Silvester

"Cats are ready to share their lives with humans as long as they can retain some freedom and some independence: they are thus distinguished from other pets. That is why some people love them and others hate them." - Hans Silvester

"The cat, when they let him out alone to do his business, never crossed the invisible line that separated the road from the dead-end." - Georges Simenon

"I would gladly change places with any of my cats." - George Ney

"A plate is distasteful to a cat, a newspaper still worse, they like to eat sticky pieces of meat sitting on a cushioned chair or a nice Persian rug." - Margaret Benson

"Whenever I see a cat in the sun, I think of humanity." - Fernando Pessoa

"When you want to hold a cat that was injured, he scratches and runs away." - Marcelle Sauvageot

"In reality, cats are probably better off remaining indoors and sending out their humans to deal with the outside world." - Dr. Phyllis Sherman Raschke

"You cannot have a better life than cats: they do what they want, when they want, as much as they want." - Ricardo Philips

"I think I'll come back as a cat." - George Ney

"His amiable amber eyes
Are very friendly, very wise;
Like Buddha, grave and fat,
He sits, regardless of applause,
And thinking, as he kneads his paws,
What fun to be a cat!" - Christopher Morley

"Cats are oppressed, dogs terrify them, landladies starve them, boys stone them, everybody speaks of them with contempt. If they were human beings we could talk of their oppressors with a studied violence, add our strength to theirs, even organize the oppressed and like good politicians sell our charity for power." - William Butler Yeats

"To be reminded that one is very much like other members of the animal kingdom is often funny...though...I do not too much mind being somewhat like a cat." - Joseph Wood Krutch

"I think it would be great to be a cat! You come and go as you please. People always feed and pet you. They don't expect much of you. You can play with them, and when you've had enough, you go away. You can pick and choose who you want to be around. You can't ask for more than that." - Patricia McPherson

"It is better, under certain circumstances to be a cat than to be a duchess...no duchess of the realm ever had more faithful retainers or half so abject subjects." - Helen M Winslow

"Among human beings a cat is just a cat; among cats a cat is a prowling shadow in a jungle." - Karel Capek

"A charm of cats is that they seem to live in a world of their own, just as much as if it were a real dimension of space." - Harriet Prescott Spofford

"Cats do not need to be shown how to have a good time, for they are unfailing ingenious in that respect." - James Mason

"Essentially, you do not so much teach your cat as bribe him." - Lynn Hollyn

"Just as the would-be debutante will fret and fuss over every detail till all is perfect, so will the fastidious feline patiently toil until every whiskertip is in place." - Lynn Hollyn

"Cats know how to obtain food without labor - shelter without confinement - and love without penalties." - W L George

"Cats are... an oxymoron. Soft, but with claws." - O B Wright

"Cats do not like anything that seems to appear as subjection and they prize the independence in which they are born." - Paul Scarron

"You may own a cat, but cannot govern one." - Kate Sanborn

"He seems the incarnation of everything soft and silky and velvety, without a sharp edge in his composition, a dreamer whose philosophy is sleep and let sleep." - Saki

"There once were two men who went to a judge about a mother cat and her kitten which they both claimed to be theirs. The judge demanded that this cat be set free between their two houses and, depending on which one of the houses she chose, the chosen house would be her master's. And all the people got excited, and I got excited with them. But the cat did not go to either house." - Imam Shafi'i

"A cat knows how to anticipate." - Roger Caras

"All cats like being the focus of attention." - Peter
Gray

"There are people who reshape the world by force or argument, but the cat just lies there, dozing, and the world quietly reshapes itself to suit his comfort and convenience." - Allen and Ivy Dodd

"A cat cares for you only as a source of food, security and a place in the sun. Her high self-sufficiency is her charm." - Charles Horton Cooley

"I think one reason we admire cats, those of us who do, is their proficiency in one-upmanship. They always seem to come out on top, no matter what they are doing - or pretend to do. Rarely do you see a cat discomfited. They have no conscience, and they never regret. Maybe we secretly envy them." - Barbara Webster

"A cat is a Regency gentleman - elegant of pose, exquisite of manner, with spotless linen and an enthusiasm for bare knuckle fights, rampaging love affairs, duels by moonlight and the singing of glees. He expects immaculate service from his domestic staff, and possesses a range of invective that would make a navvy blanch." - Pam Brown

"A wanderer himself, he is full of reproaches if I am gone beyond the expected time, yet plays with my anxieties when he is late, drifting slowly out of the darkness as if he cannot hear my calling." - Samantha Armstrong

"A cat refuses to be the object of sentimentality - if she doesn't want to be cuddled, that's it." - Samantha Armstrong

"A cat... plays for her own enjoyment, in a self-contained way, with no desire to share. Shut her up alone, and a ball, a fringe, or a looped piece of string is enough to make her give herself up to silent and graceful sport. While she is playing she does not say, 'Man, I'm so awfully glad I've got you here!' She will play beside the bed of a corpse." - Karel Capek

"The cat is not in the long run anxious to please." - T O Beachcroft

"Movement is terribly important to a cat... Nothing works quite so well as an object of jumpable size moving away. For cats, that is virtually impossible to resist." - Roger Caras

"Confront a cat with something he has never seen before and his first reaction will almost invariably be one not of fear but of curiosity." - Michael Joseph

"Cats are like the French: meals are very important to them, and they want to savour the experience without interruptions." - Kim Campbell Thornton

The Philosophy of Cats

"Everything I know I learned from my cat: When you're hungry, eat. When you're tired, nap in a sunbeam. When you go to the vets, pee on your owner." - Gary Smith

"All is well that ends well in the world of cats." - Jacques Sternberg

"It is in the nature of cats to do a certain amount of unescorted roaming." - Adlai Stevenson

"I have studied many philosophers and many cats. The wisdom of cats is infinitely superior." - Hippolyte Taine

"The motto of the cat: no matter what you did, still try to pretend that it is the fault of the dog." - Jeff Valdez

"I have studied many philosophers and many cats. The wisdom of cats is infinitely superior." - Hippolyte Taine

"All you have to remember is Rule 1: When in doubt - Wash." - Paul Gallico

"Cats seem to go on the principle that it never does any harm to ask for what you want." - Joseph Wood Krutch

"I have lived with several Zen masters, all of them cats." - Eckhart Tolle

"The only thing a cat worries about is what's happening right now. As we tell the kittens, you can only wash one paw at a time." - Lloyd Alexander, Time Cat

"Who among us hasn't envied a cat's ability to ignore the cares of daily life and to relax completely?" - Karen Brademeyer

"Letmeoutletme
outletmeoutletmeout.
Wait-let me back in!" - Lee Wardlaw, Won-Ton: A Cat Tale Told in Haiku

"Cleanliness in the cat world is usually a virtue put above godliness." - Carl Van Vechten

"A cat pretends to sleep that it may see the more clearly..." - Francois Rene, Vicomte De Chateaubriand

"Cats have a scam going - you buy the food, they eat the food, they go away; that's the deal." - Eddie Izzard

"To a cat, 'NO!' means 'Not while I'm looking'." -
Unknown

"If you say 'Hallelujah' to a cat, it will excite no fixed set of fibres in connection with any other set and the cat will exhibit none of the phenomena of consciousness. But if you say 'Me-e-at', the cat will be there in a moment..." - Samuel Butler

"Like all pure creatures, cats are practical." - William S Burroughs

"Every life should have nine cats." - Unknown

"More than likely it was the cat who first coined and put into practice the sage advice: 'If you would have a thing done well, you must do it yourself.'" - Lawrence N Johnson

"In reality, cats are probably better off remaining indoors and sending out their humans to deal with the outside world." - Dr Phyllis Sherman Raschke

"Are cats lazy? Well, more power to them if they are. Which one of us has not entertained the dream of doing just as he likes, when and how he likes, and as much as he likes?" - Fernand Mery

"He has become a much better cat than I have a person. With his gentle urgings, he made me realize that life doesn't end just because one has a few obstacles to overcome." - Mary F Graf

"If you would know what a cat is thinking about, you must hold its paw in your hand for a long time."
- Jules Champfleury

"Guilt isn't in cat vocabulary. They never suffer remorse for eating too much, sleeping too long or hogging the warmest cushion in the house. They welcome every pleasurable moment as it unravels and savour it to the full until a butterfly or falling leaf diverts their attention. They don't waste energy counting the number of calories they've consumed or the hours they've frittered away sunbathing.

Cats don't beat themselves up about not working hard enough. They don't get up and go, they sit down and stay. For them, lethargy is an art form. From their vantage points on top of fences and window ledges, they see the treadmills of human obligations for what they are - a meaningless waste of nap time." - Helen Brown, Cleo

"Cats pride themselves on their ability to do nothing." - John R F Breen

"It's a philosophical animal... one that does not place its affections thoughtlessly." - Theophile Gautier

"Cats have a consuming passion for watching human beings." - Akif Pirincci and Rolf Degen

"The cat lets Man support her. But unlike the dog, she is no handlicker. Furthermore, unlike Man's other great good friend the horse, the cat is no swearing serf of Man. The only labor she condescends to perform is to catch mice and rats and that's fun." - Vance Packard

"He seems the incarnation of everything soft and silky and velvety, without a sharp edge in his composition, a dreamer whose philosophy is sleep and let sleep." - Saki

"The great charm of cats is their rampant egotism, their devil-may-care attitude toward responsibility, their disinclination to earn an honest dollar." - Robertson Davies

"Any cat who misses a mouse pretends it was aiming for the dead leaf." - Charlotte Gray

"Tobermory looked squarely at her for a moment and then fixed his gaze serenely on the middle distance. It was obvious that boring questions like that lay outside his scheme of life." - Saki

"Cat sentimentality is a human thing. Cats are indifferent, their minds can't comprehend the concept 'I shall die,' they just go on living." - Gavin Ewart

"When addressed, a gentleman cat does not move a muscle. He looks as if he hasn't heard." - May Sarton

"Cat properties are like ranches. The space enclosed by the cat's boundaries is actually the grazing land for livestock, whether deer or deer mice, which belong to the owner and no one else, and which the owner does not disturb except to harvest." - Elizabeth Marshall Thomas

"Cats have loving hearts. But they also have self-respect, and a tendency to love only that which is lovable. It is this trait which their human masters cannot forgive." - Dorothy Canfield Fisher

"Cats... appear to regard human beings who may be domiciled with them rather as part of the furniture than as comrades." - Louis Robinson

"A cat cannot be said to have any politics. Yet it is always polite. In its outlook is the ultimate and final egoism; yet it is always a charming companion." - T O Beachcroft

"One reason that cats are happier than people is that they have no newspapers." - Gwendolyn Brooks, In the Mecca

"I'm not sitting around doing nothing. I'm busy petting the cat. Why hasn't anybody told the philosophers that this is the meaning of life?" - Jarod Kintz, Sleepwalking is Restercise

"The cat lives alone. He has no need of society. He obeys only when he wishes, he pretends to sleep the better to see, and scratches everything he can scratch." - Francois-Rene

"Cats are like donkeys and camels, they won't ever quite give in to human tyranny, they won't try to imitate the
human soul." - Richard Aldington

Proverbially Speaking...

In a cat's eye, all things belong to cats. - English Proverb

Beware of people who dislike cats. - Irish Proverb

You will always be lucky if you know how to make friends with strange cats. - Colonial American Proverb

If stretching were wealth, the cat would be rich. - African Proverb

An old cat will not learn how to dance. - Moroccan Proverb

After dark all cats are leopards. - Native American Proverb

I gave an order to a cat, and the cat gave it to its tail. - Chinese Proverb

Cats, flies and women are ever at their toilets. - French Proverb

The dog for the man, the cat for the woman. - English Proverb

Happy owner, happy cat. Indifferent owner, reclusive cat. - Chinese Proverb

A cat has nine lives. For three he plays, for three he strays, and for the last three he stays. - English Proverb

Happy is the home with at least one cat. - Italian Proverb

The cat was created when the lion sneezed. - Arabian Proverb

Curiosity killed the cat, Satisfaction brought it back! - English Proverb

Books and cats and fair-haired little girls make the best furnishing for a room. - French Proverb

The cat who frightens the mice away is as good as the cat who eats them. - German proverb

A cat bitten once by a snake dreads even rope. - Arab Proverb

A cat may go to a monastery, but she still remains a cat. - Ethiopian proverb

The dog may be wonderful prose, but only the cat is poetry. - French Proverb

A cat is a lion in a jungle of small bushes. - Indian Proverb

Those that dislike cats will be carried to the cemetery in the rain. - Dutch Proverb

If stretching were wealth, the cat would be rich. -
African Proverb

Old cats mean young mice. - Italian proverb

An old cat will not learn dancing. - Moroccan
Proverb

When the cat and mouse agree, the grocer is ruined.
- Iranian Proverb

The kind man feeds his beast before sitting down to
dinner. - Hebrew Proverb

The cat loves fish, but hates wet feet. - Medieval
Proverb

The cat dreams of garbage. - Hindu Proverb

It is better to be a mouse in a cat's mouth than a man
in a lawyer's hands. - Spanish Proverb

The cat always leaves a mark on his friend. -
Spanish Proverb

The cat wonders at its own tail. - Spanish Proverb

To kill a cat brings seventeen years of bad luck. -
Irish Proverb

Handsome cats and fat dungheaps are the sign of a
good farmer. - French Proverb

My soul feels as disturbed as if a cat were treading my heart. - Chinese Proverb

Dogs remember faces, cats places. - English Proverb

An overdressed woman is like a cat dressed in saffron. - Egyptian Proverb

When moving to a new home, always put the cat through the window instead of the door, so that it will not leave. - American Proverb

A cat's a cat and that's that. - American Proverb

It is better to feed one cat than many mice. - Norwegian Proverb

He who makes a mouse of himself, will be eaten by the cats. - German Proverb

Two cats can never be equal; one will always be bigger than the other. - African Proverb

Fine words don't feed cats. - Italian Proverb

He who hunts with cats will catch mice. - Danish Proverb

Wanton kittens make sober cats. - Danish Proverb

A peasant between two lawyers is like a fish between two cats. - Spanish Proverb

Who cares well for cats will marry as happily as he or she could ever wish. - French Proverb

All cats are bad in May. - French Proverb

Women are just like cats - they always land on their feet. - Persian Proverb

Rocking chairs make long-tailed cats uneasy. - Mexican Proverb

The dream of cats is all mice. - Egyptian Proverb

In a place without dogs they teach the cats to bark. - Georgian Proverb

No matter how much the world changes, cats will never lay eggs. - Bambara Proverb

He who is a little cat outside is a little dog at home. - Estonian Proverb

Cat will eventually get a downpour of mice's tears. - Russian Proverb

Wait for the cat to jump. - English Proverb

Blind cat's prayers bring no rain. - Persian Proverb

Cats hide their claws. - English Proverb

A rat who gnaws at a cat's tail invites destruction. - Chinese Proverb

The three merriest things in the world are a cat's kitten, a goat's kid, and a young widow. - Irish Proverb

It is for her own good that the cat purrs. - Irish Proverb

A bon chat bon rat. (A good cat deserves a good rat.) - French Proverb

The kind man feeds his cat before sitting down to dinner. - Hebrew Proverb

When the mouse laughs at the cat, there's a hole nearby. - Nigerian Proverb

I gave an order to a cat, and the cat gave it to its tail. - Chinese Proverb

When rats infest the Palace a lame cat is better than the swiftest horse. - Chinese Proverb

You can't trust a cat to guard the cream. - English Proverb

It is like a cat drinking milk with its eyes closed. - Indian Proverb

If the cat has to die, let it die full. - Galicien Proverb

A dried fish cannot be used as a cat's pillow. -
Chinese Proverb

If you don't have a dog, you hunt with a cat. - Portuguese Proverb

Even a cat appreciates kind words. - Russian Proverb

The cat knows who's meat it has eaten. - Russian Proverb

The gentle cat scratches the worst. - Romanian Proverb

A cat that is hidden with its tail showing. - Portuguese Proverb

Go slowly, come slowly, lest the cat should gore you. - Persian Proverb

It's enough to make a cat laugh. - English Proverb

After dark, all cats are leopards. - Zuni Proverb

What can a cat do if its master is crazy? - Corsican Proverb

Every cat has a proper tail. Over there is a cat with no tail. - Corsican Proverb

Cats always fall on their paws. - Spanish Proverb

Beware of the cat that licks from the front but claws from behind. - English Proverb

Who would believe such pleasure from a wee ball o'fur? - Irish Proverb

Slogans and Puns

"Tastes so good cats ask for it by name" - Meowmix slogan

"Eight out of ten cats prefer it." - Whiskas

"Cats like Felix like Felix." - Felix

"Cats know the difference." - Whiskas

"A real treat for your cat's teeth." - Whiskas Dentabits

"For cats with an appetite for life." - Friskies Go-Cat

"Good taste is easy to recognize." - Fancy Feast

"Sheba. To say I love you." - Sheba

"A language you both understand." - Friskies Go-Cat

"Friskies. For more." - Friskies Go-Cat

"Cats would buy Whiskas if they could." - Whiskas

"Real taste. Real excitement." - 9 Lives

"The cat who doesn't act finicky soon loses control of his owner." - 9 Lives

"Real Men Love Cats." - T-shirt

"Cat Hair Shirt" - T-shirt

"Claws for Alarm" - Nick and Nora Mysteries, TC LoTempio

"Pouncing on Murder." - A Bookmobile Cat Mystery, Laurie Cass

"Paws and Effect." - A Magical Cats Mystery, Sofie Kelly

"A Midwinter's Tail." - A Magical Cats Mystery, Sofie Kelly

"Fat Cat Takes the Cake." - A Fat Cat Mystery, Janet Cantrell

"The Whole Cat and Caboodle." - Second Chance Cat Mystery, Sofie Ryan

"A Deadly Tail." - Whiskey Tango Foxtrot Mystery, Dixie Lyle

"Purrfectly Dead." - Whiskey Tango Foxtrot Mystery, Dixie Lyle

"Catch as Cat Can." - A Sunny and Shadow Mystery, Claire Donnally

"Hiss and Tell." - Novel Ideas Mysteries, Lucy Arlington

"What do cats eat for breakfast? Mice krispies." - Unknown

"Did you hear about the cat who swallowed a ball of wool? She had mittens." - Unknown

"How did a cat take first prize at a bird show? He just jumped up to the cage, reached in, and took it." - Unknown

"How does a cat keep law and order? Claw enforcement." - Unknown

"What do you call the cat that was caught by the police? The purrpatrator." - Unknown

"What kind of car does a cat drive? A Furr-rarai." - Unknown

"What do you call a cat that addresses the media? A press kit." - Unknown

"Where does a cat go if he loses his tail? The retail store." - Unknown

"What do you call a cat that has swallowed a duck? A duck-filled fatty puss." - Unknown

"Why can't cats play poker in the jungle? Too many cheetahs." - Unknown

"What's a cat's favourite colour? Purrrr-ple." - Unknown

"What happened when the cat went to the flea circus? He stole the whole show." - Unknown

"Why is it hard for a leopard to hide? Because he's always spotted." - Unknown

"What kind of cat will keep your grass short? A lawn meower." - Unknown

"What type of cats purr more than others? Purr-sians." - Unknown

"What did the cat say when he bit his tail? That's the end of me." - Unknown

"If a big cat is a flabby tabby, then what is a very small cat? An itty bitty kitty." - Unknown

"What did one cat say to the other? Have you heard the mews today?" - Unknown

"What do feline actors say on stage? Tabby or not tabby?" - Unknown

"Why did the cat eat the cheese? So he could sit by the mouse hole with baited breath." - Unknown

"What do you get if you cross a tomcat with a Pekinese? A Peking Tom." - Unknown

"What do you call a cat that eats lemons? A sour puss." - Unknown

"What is the difference between a cat and a comma? One has the paws before the claws and the other has the clause before the pause." - Unknown

"What's a cat's favourite dessert? Chocolate Mouse." - Unknown

"What do you call a pile of kittens? A meowtain." - Unknown

"What do you get if you cross a cat with a dark horse? Kitty Perry." - Unknown

"What do you call a lion who has eaten your mother's sister? An aunt-eater." - Unknown

"You've cat to be kitten me right meow." - Jackson Galaxy

"Why do people love cats so much? Because they are purr-fect." - Unknown

"Catification." - Jackson Galaxy

"Catify to Satisfy." - Jackson Galaxy

"Cat puns freak meowt." - Killarney Cat Hospital

"Cat puns fur-ever." - Unknown

**SPECIAL SECTION
OFFICIAL CRAZY CAT PEOPLE
HALL OF FAME**

NEIL GAIMAN

Neil Gaiman photo by Kyle Cassidy in April 2013.

It will come as no surprise to anybody who regularly reads the work of author Neil Gaiman that he would describe himself as "a cat person." Cats seem to slink their way into many of his stories, for example in 'The Season of Mists', the ancient Egyptian cat goddess Bastet mourns the loss of her popularity, and in a heartwarming tale called 'The Price' he writes about rescuing a black cat in what starts off seeming like an autobiographical story. In the end, the stray saves him from a female incarnation of the devil, which presumably didn't happen, although knowing Neil, who knows?

"There are those who have suggested that the tendency of a cat to play with its prey is a merciful one..."
- Neil Gaiman, Coraline

"No," said the cat. "Now, you people have names. That's because you don't know who you are. We know who we are, so we don't need names."
- Neil Gaiman, Coraline

"Cats don't have names," it said.

"No?" said Coraline.

"No," said the cat. "Now, you people have names. That's because you don't know who you are. We know who we are, so we don't need names."

There was something irritatingly self-centered about the cat, Coraline decided. As if it were, in its opinion, the only thing in any world or place that could possibly be of any importance.

Half of her wanted to be very rude to it; the other half of her wanted to be polite and deferential. The polite half won."
- Neil Gaiman, Coraline

"But there was a kitten on my pillow, and it was purring in my face and vibrating gently with every purr, and, very soon, I slept."
- Neil Gaiman, The Ocean at the End of the Lane

"The ball of dark fur pressed itself into my chest, and I wished she was my kitten, and knew that she was not."
- Neil Gaiman, The Ocean at the End of the Lane

"I would like to see anyone, prophet, king or God, convince a thousand cats to do the same thing at the same time."
- Neil Gaiman

"Anyone who believes what a cat tells him deserves all he gets."
- Neil Gaiman, Stardust

"Now you people have names. That's because you don't know who you are. We know who we are, so we don't need names."
- Neil Gaiman, Coraline

"The cat wrinkled its nose and managed to look unimpressed. "Calling cats," it confided, "tends to be a rather overrated activity. Might as well call a whirlwind."
- Neil Gaiman, Coraline

"We never seem to have more than eight cats, rarely have less than three." - Neil Gaiman, The Price

"The cat dropped the rat between its two front paws. "There are those," it said with a sigh, in tones as smooth as oiled silk, "who have suggested that the tendency of a cat to play with its prey is a merciful one - after all, it permits the occasional funny little running snack to escape, from time to time. How often does your dinner get to escape?"
- Neil Gaiman, Coraline

"Name the different kinds of people,' said Miss Lupescu. 'Now.'
Bod thought for a moment. 'The living,' he said. 'Er. The dead.' He stopped. Then, '... Cats?' he offered, uncertainly."
- Neil Gaiman, The Graveyard Book

"Tramps and vagabonds have marks they make on gateposts and trees and doors, letting others of their kind know a little about the people who live at the houses and farms they pass on their travels. I think cats must leave similar signs; how else to explain the cats who turn up at our door through the year,

hungry and flea-ridden and abandoned?" - Neil
Gaiman, the Price

"Some animals are survivors." - Neil Gaiman,
online Journal

"Princess is the oldest cat we have. She arrived here
on June the 26th 1994, Holly's 9th birthday, but I'd
glimpsed her at a distance, a feral ghost living wild
in the woods for a good year before that. She's
feisty and grumpy and likes making people do their
trick for her, which is turning on the tap so a trickle
of water comes out, and then waiting while she
drinks a little. She glares at you if you turn the tap
off before she's done." - Neil Gaiman, online
journal

TERRY PRATCHETT

Prolific author Terry Pratchett was also well known for his love of felines. In his Discworld series, the character of Death is particularly fond of kitties, and when asked by one person what the point of life was, famously answered "Cats? Cats are nice." Terry also dedicated an entire non-fiction humour book to his favourite animals, titled 'The Unadulterated Cat', which was first published by Gollancz in 1989. It is said that his cat, along with his family, were by his side when he died in 2015.

"Maurice watched them argue again. Humans, eh? Think they're lords of creation. Not like us cats. We know we are. Ever see a cat feed a human? Case proven." - Terry Pratchett, The Amazing Maurice and His Educated Rodents

"Dogs are not like cats, who amusingly tolerate humans only until someone comes up with a tin opener that can be operated with a paw. Men made dogs, they took wolves and gave them human things-unnecessary intelligence, names, a desire to belong, and a twitching inferiority complex. All dogs dream wolf dreams, and know they're dreaming of biting their Maker. Every dog knows, deep in his heart, that he is a Bad Dog..." - Terry Pratchett, Men at Arms

"WHAT FOR IS THIS BOX PADDED? IS IT TO BE SAT ON? CAN IT BE THAT IT IS CAT-FLAVOURED?" - Terry Pratchett, Reaper Man

"Witches were a bit like cats. They didn't much like one another's company but they did like to know where all the other witches were, just in case they needed them. And what you might need them for was to tell you, as a friend, that you were beginning to cackle." - Terry Pratchett, A Hat Full of Sky

"Cats do not hunt seals. They would hunt them if they knew what seals and where to find them. But they do not know, so it's okay." - Terry Pratchett

"Witches were a bit like cats. They didn't much like one another's company, but they did like to know where all the other witches were, just in case they needed them." - Terry Pratchett, A Hat Full of Sky

"If cats looked like frogs we'd realize what nasty, cruel little bastards they are. Style. That's what people remember." - Terry Pratchett, Lords and Ladies

"I meant," said Ipslore bitterly, "what is there in this world that truly makes living worthwhile?"
Death thought about it.
CATS, he said eventually. CATS ARE NICE." - Terry Pratchett, Sourcery

"I DON'T HOLD WITH CRUELTY TO CATS." - Terry Pratchett, The Last Hero

"And then there were cats, thought Dog. He'd surprised the huge ginger cat from next door and had attempted to reduce it to cowering jelly by

means of the usual glowing stare and deep-throated growl, which had always worked on the damned in the past. This time they had earned him a whack on the nose that had made his eyes water. Cats, Dog considered, were clearly a lot tougher than lost souls. He was looking forward to a further cat experiment, which he planned would consist of jumping around and yapping excitedly at it. It was a long shot, but it just might work."
- Terry Pratchett, Good Omens: The Nice and Accurate Prophecies of Agnes Nutter, Witch

"Cats will amusingly tolerate humans only until someone comes up with a tin opener that can be operated with a paw."
- Terry Pratchett, Men at Arms

"'I hate cats.'
Death's face became a little stiffer, if that were possible. The blue glow in his eye sockets flickered red for an instant.
'I SEE,' he said. The tone suggested that death was too good for cat haters." - Terry Pratchett, Wyrd Sisters

"Cats gravitate to kitchens like rocks gravitate to gravity." - Terry Pratchett, Witches Abroad

"Maurice watched them argue again. Humans, eh? Think they're lords of creation. Not like us cats. We know we are. Ever see a cat feed a human? Case proven." - Terry Pratchett, The Amazing Maurice and His Educated Rodents

"Dogs are not like cats, who amusingly tolerate humans only until someone comes up with a tin opener that can be operated with a paw. Men made dogs, they took wolves and gave them human things-unnecessary intelligence, names, a desire to belong, and a twitching inferiority complex. All dogs dream wolf dreams, and know they're dreaming of biting their Maker. Every dog knows, deep in his heart, that he is a Bad Dog..." - Terry Pratchett, Men at Arms

"It's an interesting fact that fewer than 17 % of Real cats end their lives with the same name they started with. Much family effort goes into selecting one at the start ("She looks like a Winnifred to me"), and the as the years roll by it suddenly finds itself being called Meepo or Ratbag." - Terry Pratchett, The Unadulterated Cat

"Our garden was debated territory between five local cats, and we'd heard that the best way to keep other cats out of the garden was to have one yourself. A moment's rational thought here will spot the slight flaw in this reasoning." - Terry Pratchett, The Unadulterated Cat

"If cats looked like frogs we'd realize what nasty, cruel little bastards they are. Style. That's what people remember." - Terry Pratchett, Lords and Ladies

DORIS LESSING

Doris Lessing photo by Elke Wetzig (elya).

The late author Doris Lessing is another who was famously enchanted by cats. She wrote 'On Cats' about the cats she had loved throughout her life, including two who particularly made their mark, Rufus the Survivor and El Magnifico. Cats also feature in her fiction, particularly 'An Old Woman and her Cat' which tells the tale of a lonely old lady whose only solace is her tom cat. However, Doris' work comes with a warning, some people might find it brutal and there are rarely happy endings or sugar coatings - she certainly pulls no punches in her stories.

"Her ears, lightly fringed with white that looked silver, lifted and moved, back, forward, listening and sensing. Her face turned, slightly, after each new sensation, alert. Her tail moved, in another dimension, as if its tip was catching messages her other organs could not. She sat poised, air-light, looking, hearing, feeling, smelling, breathing, with all of her, fur, whiskers, ears - everything, in delicate vibration." - Doris Lessing, On Cats

"Hetty's life from the coming of the cat became more sociable, for the beast was always making friends with somebody in the cliff that was the block of flats across the court, or not coming home for nights at a time so that she had to go and look for him and knock on doors and ask, or returning home kicked and limping, or bleeding after a fight with his kind." - Doris Lessing, An Old Woman And Her Cat

"The cat was soon a scarred warrior with fleas, a torn ear, and a ragged look to him. He was a multicoloured cat and his eyes were small and yellow. He was a long way down the scale from the delicately coloured, elegantly shaped pedigree cats." - Doris Lessing, An Old Woman And Her Cat

"Cats mean kittens, plentiful and frequent." - Doris Lessing, On Cats

"But now, remembering cats, always cats, a hundred incidents involving cats, years and years of cats, I am astounded at the hard work they must have meant. In London now I have two cats; and often enough I say, What nonsense that one should have all this trouble and worry on account of two small animals." - Doris Lessing, On Cats

"That was it. Never again. And for years I matched cats in friends' houses, cats in shops, cats on farms, cats in the street, cats on walls, cats in memory, with that gentle blue-grey purring creature which for me was the cat, the Cat, never to be replaced." - Doris Lessing, On Cats

"For a few months a large black cat lived on the staircase of the flats, belonging, apparently, to nobody. It wanted to belong to one of us." - Doris Lessing, On Cats

"Our cat, the princess, was, still is, beautiful, but, there is no glossing it, she's a selfish beast." - Doris Lessing, On Cats

"Knowing cats, a lifetime of cats, what is left is a sediment of sorrow quite different from that due to humans: compounded of pain, for their helplessness, of guilt on behalf of us all." - Doris Lessing

"What a luxury a cat is, the moments of shocking and startling pleasure in a day, the feel of the beast, the soft sleekness under your palm, the warmth when you wake on a cold night, the grace and charm even in a quite ordinary workaday puss. Cat walks across your room, and in that lonely stalk you see leopard or even panther, or it turns its head to acknowledge you and the yellow blaze of those eyes tells you what an exotic visitor you have here, in this household friend, the cat who purrs as you stroke, or rub his chin, or scratch his head." - Doris Lessing

"I knew that there would be a cat in the house. Just as one knows, if a house is too large people will come and live in it, so certain houses must have cats." - Doris Lessing

MARGARET ATWOOD

Margaret Atwood publicity photo by Jean Malek.

Canadian author Margaret Atwood is another official cat fan deserving of an entry in this hall of fame. Although cats have never held a starring role in any of her full-length fiction, in her recent MaddAddam sci-fi trilogy, a new species is created called the Crakers which are essentially hybrid humans that share some cat characteristics, including being able to purr at a certain sound frequency that allows them to heal themselves. Margaret also sometimes writes poems which feature her cats, like 'Blackie in Antarctica' and 'February.'

"In the pewter mornings, the cat,
a black fur sausage with yellow
Houdini eyes, jumps up on the bed and tries
to get onto my head. It's his
way of telling whether or not I'm dead." - Margaret Atwood, February

"'Meow', said our cat.
'Meow', said God. Actually it was more like a roar.
'I always thought you were a cat', said our cat, 'but I wasn't sure'." -Margaret Atwood, Our Cat Enters Heaven

"Nobody quite knows the truth about cats purring, but it does seem to be also a self-healing thing for them, which is why, when you take your cat to the vet and it's frightened, it will purr." - Margaret Atwood, Interview with MacLeans, Brian Bethune August 24, 2013

"There's more than one cat in any bag." - Margaret Atwood, Lady Oracle

"Should you have a migraine," she said, "put a cat on your head. How you will keep it there is another question." - Margaret Atwood

"Cat-like, you hated being ridiculous." - Margaret Atwood, Blackie in Antarctica

"Why do dead cats
call up such ludicrous tears?
Why such deep mourning?
Because we can no longer
see in the dark without them?
Because we're cold
without their fur?" - Margaret Atwood, Mourning for Cats

"I'm too black and ugly for him, plus he just likes the kittens, not the old cats. Maybe you should wrinkle yourself up, sweetheart." - Margaret Atwood, The Year Of The Flood

"She's always been aware of other people's awareness, she was like a cat." - Margaret Atwood, The Year Of The Flood

"Cats of all kinds will set ambushes: one frisks around in the open to distract your attention while another one slips quietly up behind." - Margaret Atwood, The Year Of The Flood

"Snowman has a hurt foot. We purred over it, but it needs more purring." - Margaret Atwood, The Year Of The Flood

"Three Crakers are purring over him, taking turns: two men and a woman, gold, ivory, ebony. It's a different three every few hours. Do they have only so much purring quotient, are they like batteries that need to be recharged? Naturally they need time off to graze and water themselves, but does the purring itself have a sort of electrical frequency?" - Margaret Atwood, MaddAddam

"Thank you for the purring. I am not feeling so sick now." - Margaret Atwood, MaddAddam

"Dropbox. What is it? Nothing comes to mind but an indoor cat-poo station. But he won't ask." - Margaret Atwood, The Stone Mattress

"At night, sleepless, I would roam the house, listening to the snores of the others, their yelps of nightmare. The cat kept me company. It was the only living creature that wanted to be close to me." - Margaret Atwood, The Stone Mattress

"He wasn't looking forward to the publication of his own book - too many cats would come swarming out of the bag." - Margaret Atwood, The Stone Mattress

"Useless to stay in his room, to try to work; at his desk he will only doze, but with his ears alert, like a drowsing cat's, attuned to the sound of footsteps on the stairs." - Margaret Atwood, Alias Grace

"I tackled each step at a time, hugging the banister; then along the hall to the kitchen, the fingers of my left hand brushing the wall like a cat's whiskers." - Margaret Atwood, The Blind Assassin

"His voice was what was called a whisky voice - low, deep almost, with a rough, scraped overlay to it like a cat's tongue - like velvet made of leather." - Margaret Atwood, The Blind Assassin

"They don't have a cat, but she's bloody well going to get one and charge it to Nate." - Margaret Atwood, Life Before Man

"He did what he thought was expected of him, and brought the official pieces of paper home to her like a cat bringing dead mice." - Margaret Atwood, The Robber Bride

"Thus padded, she takes a breath, clenches all her flesh together, and heads through the door, into the winter. The cat shoots out between her legs and immediately thinks better of it. Marcia lets it back in." - Margaret Atwood, Wilderness Tips

"Cats prowl around in there, we see them every day, crouching, squatting, scratching up the dirt, staring out at us with their yellow eyes as if we're something they're hunting." - Margaret Atwood, Cat's Eye

"Mr Banerji says he hears there is now a naked cat available, he's read about it in a magazine, though he himself does not see the point of it at all." - Margaret Atwood, Cat's Eye

"In the soft green drizzle my cat crosses the street." - Margaret Atwood, Good Bones and Simple Murders

"There's no point trying to work, Moira won't allow it, she's like a cat that crawls onto the page when you're trying to read." - Margaret Atwood, The Handmaid's Tale

"There was an abnormal number of cats." - Margaret Atwood, The Edible Woman

CATWOMAN

Probably the best comic book villain ever, the sexy Catwoman is one of superhero Batman's constant enemies within the city of Gotham. She's been there since the very beginning, and made her debut in Batman#1, created by Bob Kane and Bill Finger. She was originally known as simply 'the cat' and much later was given the human name of Selina Kyle. Her day job is a high-stakes thief and her relationship with Batman has evolved over the years and is now probably best described as... complicated.

"I am Catwoman. Hear me roar." - Catwoman, Batman Returns

"You're catnip to a girl like me. Handsome, dazed, and to die for." - Catwoman, Batman Returns

"Please. I wouldn't touch you to scratch you." - Catwoman, Batman Returns

[after falling into an open gravel filled truck] "Saved by kitty litter." - Catwoman, Batman Returns

"Cats come when they feel like it. Not when they're told." - Catwoman

You're going to see the purr-fect crime, when I get Batman in my claws! - Catwoman, Batman: The Movie

"'Penguin, you know I can't take water!' 'You cowardly kitten! You want to live forever?'" - Catwoman, Batman: The Movie

"Amber Forever: 'You're Catwoman!' Catwoman: 'In the fur.' - Catwoman, Batman: Batman Displays His Knowledge

"When we complete this caper, we're gonna have enough money to keep us in catnip forever." - Catwoman, Batman: The Cat's Meow

"Fresh catnip? At THIS time of night?" - Catwoman, Batman: The Sandman Cometh

"Robin: 'Don't fret. With good behavior, you could be out in seven-and-a-half years.' Catwoman: [sadly] 'I'll be an old tabby by then'." - Catwoman, Batman: The Cat and the Fiddle

"Rabbiting? I've never rabbited in my life! I've pussy-footed. I've cat-scratched. I've even kittycornered. But I don't rabbit!" - Catwoman Vol.2 #12

"They may suspect me, but they'll never see me. They may chase me, but they'll never catch me. Never, never, ever catch me." - Catwoman Vol.2 #19

"You are part of the night, just like me. We're not afraid of the dark-we come alive in it...we're thrilled by it." [to Batman] - Catwoman Vol.2 #40

"A long time ago, before I put on this mask, I was afraid of everything." - Catwoman Vol.2 #59

"That's part of the rule. Never quit. Never let them see you're afraid. Above all - never let them see you're hurt. Never let them see you cry. Never." - Catwoman Vol.2 #75

"You see, sometimes I'm good. Oh, I'm very good. But sometimes I'm bad. But only as bad as I wanna be. Freedom is power. To live a life untamed and unafraid is the gift that I've been given, and so my journey begins." - Catwoman, Catwoman (2004)

"Ophelia: 'She's an Egyptian Mau, the rarest of breeds. Temple cats. It's said that Maus have special powers.'" - Catwoman (2004)

"I don't know about you, Miss Kitty, but I feel so much... yummier." [after her first transformation into Catwoman] - Catwoman, Batman Returns (1992)

"You killed me. The Penguin killed me. Batman killed me. That's three lives down - you got enough in there to finish me off! [To Schreck] Four....five...still alive! [as her lives are being depleted by gunshots]

Six? Seven? All good girls go to heaven..." [As she is shot for the third and fourth time.] - Catwoman, Batman Returns (1992)

"[after appearing during Batman's rescue of the Ice Princess] Did someone say fish? I haven't been fed all day." - Catwoman, Batman Returns (1992)

"When it comes to reflexes, I'm like a cat. I'm Catwoman. I'm invulnerable. The only reason he got a piece of me is because of the rain. Cats don't like water. It impairs us. It's our kryptonite." - Becca Fitzpatrick, Hush, Hush

"Laurel Hedare: 'Game over!'
Catwoman: 'Guess what? It's overtime!'" - Catwoman, Catwoman (2004)

"Catwoman: 'You like bad girls?'" - Catwoman (2004)

"Catwoman: [off screen] 'If you pick the right door, I'm yours, Batman. If you pick the wrong door, you're mine. So which is it, Batman? The lady or the tiger?'" - Catwoman,
Batman: The Funny Feline Felonies (1967)

FINAL NOTE

If you love cats and have a bit of cash to spare, why not make a donation to one of the following cat charities? I know people who work for them all personally and have seen them hard at work first hand. None of them have CEOs with six-figure salaries, 'boards of directors' with bloated salaries or any such rubbish. Any money you give will genuinely go to helping down on their luck kitties.

HONEYCAT RESCUE
Based beside the seaside in Eastbourne in Sussex, Honeycat houses up to 90 cats at any one time in a specially adapted house and garden, and specializes in adopting out FIV positive felines and educating people on the disease. As you can imagine, the outgoings and effort required to keep things ticking over with 90 meowing mouths to feed is huge.
www.honeycatrescue.org

ROMNEY HOUSE CAT RESCUE
Another great rescue centre, this one based in Downe in Kent and homing cats to London and the South East, Romney House also cares for a number of 'unadoptable' cats on its sprawling premises, permanent residents with problems which mean they are unlikely to ever find a happy home. You can make a general donation or choose one of these critters to sponsor for a year.
www.romneyhousecatrescue.org.uk

NINE LIVES GREECE
A group of volunteers who look after the many, many homeless cats that roam the streets of Greece. They fund and perform trap, neuter and release programs and provide food and veterinary care for as many pussycats as they can. They also have some special cats that are up for adoption to overseas homes, providing you're promising them a happy forever home.
www.ninelivesgreece.com

SANTORINI ANIMAL WELFARE ASSOCIATION
The beautiful Greek Island of Santorini is home to many stray animals and this rescue organization helps care for them, particularly during the off season when many of the restaurants and bars close down. SAWA looks after not only stray cats, but stray dogs and donkeys, too.
www.sawasantorini.org

BIBLIOGRAPHY

Anderson, Janice. *The Cat-A-Logue*. Enfield: Guinness Books, 1987. Print.

Aveni, Mary Kate (editor). *Cats*. Carlton Books Limited, 2008.

Aveni, Mary Kate (editor). *Cats: A Photographic Celebration*. Metro Books, 2007.

Baird, David (editor). *Where Cats Meditate*. MQ Publications Limited, 2003. Print.

Beard, Henry. *Poetry For Cats: The Definitive Anthology of Distinguished Feline Verse*. HarperCollins Publishers, 1995. Print.

Becker, Marty, and Gina Spadafori. *MeowWow: Curiously Compelling Facts, True Tales, And Trivia Even Your Cat Won't Know*. Deerfield Beach, FL: Health Communications, 2007. Print.

Brandreth, Gyles. *Cats' Tales*. Robson Books Ltd, 1986. Print.

Brown, Milly. *The Cat Lover's Companion*. Summersdale Publishers Ltd, 2011.

Carr, Samuel (editor). *The Poetry of Cats*. Chancellor Press, 1986. Print.

Choron, Sandra, Harry Choron, and Arden Moore. *Planet Cat: A Cat-Alog*. Boston: Houghton Mifflin Co., 2007. Print.

Coates, Deborah. *Cat Haiku: The Ancient Art of Japanese Poetry - Cat Style*. Arrow Books, 2003. Print.

Cook, Gladys Emerson, and Felix Sutton. *The Big Book Of Cats*. New York: Grossett & Dunlap, 1954. Print.

Diego, Calif. *Uncle John's Bathroom Reader Cat Lover's Companion*. San Diego, CA: Portable Press, 2006. Print.

Edney, Andrew. *Cat: Wild Cats and Pampered Pets*. The Ivy Press Limited, 1999. Print.

Elliott, Charles (editor). *The Cat Fanatic: Quirky Quotes on Frisky Felines*. JR Books, 2007. Print.

Elliott, Charles (editor). *The Quotable Cat Lover*. Sterling Publishing Company Inc, 2004. Print.

Exley, Helen (editor). *Cats: A Celebration in Words and Paintings*. Exley Publications, 1992. Print.

Exley, Helen (editor). *Cat Quotations*. Exley Publications, 1991. Print.

Hallepee, Didier. *Cat Secrets: Over 1000 Quotes About Cats*. Createspace, 2011. Ebook.

Jacobs, David and Dunton, Trevor. *The Awfully Good Cat Joke Book*. Metro Books, 1996. Print.

MacBeth, George and Booth, Martin (editors). *The Book of Cats*. Bloodaxe Books, 1992. Print.

Mara, Lesley. *Cats Miscellany: Everything You Always Wanted To Know About Our Feline Friends*. New York: Skyhorse Pub., 2011. Print.

May, Kate. *Cat Wit: Quips and Quotes for the Feline Obsessed*. Summersdale Press, 2012. Print.

Moore, Joan. *The Cat Lover's Companion*. Montreal: Tormont, 19931992. Print.

Neill, Amanda. *Cat Biz*. Hauppauge, N.Y.: Barron's, 20072006. Print.

Ortolja-Baird, Alexandra (editor). *Cats Do The Cutest Things*. MQ Publications Limited, 2004. Print.

Rutledge, Leigh W, *A Cat's Little Instruction Book.* Penguin Group, 1993. Print.

Taylor, David and Martyn, Elizabeth. *The Little Tabby Cat Book*. Dorling Kindersley Limited, 1990.

Unknown Editor. *Adorable Cats*. SJP Publishing, 2011. Print.

Unknown Editor. *Feline Friends: A Cat Lover's Treasury*. Quercus, 2007. Print.

Unknown Editor. *The Artistic Cat: Praise, Poems and Paintings*. Running Press, 1991. Print.

Unknown Editor. *The Literary Cat: Quips, Quotes and Observations*. Running Press, 1990. Print.

Unknown Editor. *Quotable Cats*. Summersdale Press, 2006. Print.

Wardlaw, Lee and Yelchin, Eugene. *Won Ton: A Cat Tale Told in Haiku*. Henry Holt and Company, 2011. Print.

Wardlaw, Lee and Yelchin, Eugene. *Won Ton and Chopstick*. Henry Holt and Company, 2015. Print.

PICTURE CREDITS

Cat silhouettes all from Wikimedia Commons. Walking Cat Silhouette by Persian Poet Gal. Sitting Cat Silhouette by Booyabazooka. Paw print by OCAL. Stretching cat silhouette by rferran.

Cover design and photography by Damon Torsten Nash. Damon can be contacted at pwurg@hotmail.com.

Margaret Atwood publicity photo by Jean Malek. Her official web site is at http://margaretatwood.ca/

Neil Gaiman photo by Kyle Cassidy in April 2013. To keep up with Neil's cats, check out his journal at http://journal.neilgaiman.com/

Doris Lessing photo by Elke Wetzig (elya). Taken at lit.cologne, Cologne literature festival 2006, Germany.

Terry Pratchett photo by Luigi Novi. © Luigi Novi / Wikimedia Commons. Taken on Day 2 of the 2012 New York Comic Con, Friday October 12, 2012.

All other photographs by and copyright Emma Boyes or Damon Torsten Nash.

A note about accents: many of the people's names in this book are European and the correct spelling involves the use of various accents and characters, for example circumflex, cedilla and acute and grave accents over vowels. I have had to remove these as some devices appear to have problems reading them. No offence (or anglicizing of people's names) is intended and I hope my apologies will be accepted for having to do this for the sake of technical issues.

www.ingramcontent.com/pod-product-compliance
Lightning Source LLC
Chambersburg PA
CBHW061958280526
45787CB00005B/1921